MARK E. BELL

June 1976

INSPIRING OBJECT LESSONS

MA

INSPIRING OBJECT LESSONS

MARK E. BELL

by
Mark E. Bell

BAKER BOOK HOUSE
Grand Rapids, Michigan

INSPIRING OBJECT LESSONS

by

John H. Sargent

BAKER BOOK HOUSE
Grand Rapids, Michigan

Library of Congress Catalog Card Number: 61-17634

ISBN: 0-8010-7992-6

Copyright 1961 by
Baker Book House Company

Previously published as
52 Parables

PHOTOLITHOPRINTED BY CUSHING - MALLOY, INC.
ANN ARBOR, MICHIGAN, UNITED STATES OF AMERICA
1973

*I affectionately dedicate this book
to my Grandson*
BRADFORD JOHN SARGENT
*and
to my Granddaughter*
LEE ANN SARGENT

CONTENTS
Alphabetically Arranged

Parable	Page
Auxanometers	41
Baseball Bat, A	63
Bicycles	29
Blacksmith, The	73
By Your Weight	45
Candle, A	19
Charge It	47
Christmas	75
Don't Lower Your Arm	43
evol zi boP	111
Foundations	67
Held by a Tongue	53
Hornets	33
How Birds Fly	25
Hub, The	109
Ice	99
In Everything there is Music	13
It's Time to Paint	101
Ivy	23
Keep Walking	37
Key Logs	27
Light	107
Little Golf Ball, A	91
Models	35
Names	95
Ninth Inning Homer, A	79
No Sissies Here	93
Oars	89
Over the Hill	85
Pail of Water, A	59
Pearls	65
Pendulum, A	55
Power	103
Pull or Kick	49
Red Fence	9
Ruts	97

Parable	Page
Screens	39
Shingles	69
Small Stone, A	51
Sounds You Cannot Hear	11
Speck of Dust, A	57
Stethoscopes	61
Tape Recordings	37
Thanksgiving	77
Thank You God	21
Tongues	71
Wheel Barrows	15
Why Sparks Fly	81
Windshields	87
Wings	105
Yoke, A	83
Your Weight	17

THE RED FENCE

Have you ever misjudged someone? You know — thinking someone told a lie about you, and you found out later that he didn't?

Perhaps you got mad at your friend because you thought he was wrong — only later to find out that YOU were the one who was wrong.

It's like seeing a blue cow. Did you ever see a blue cow? Well I did once! But, actually she only appeared to me to be blue because I had a pair of blue tinted sun glasses on!

Not long ago while riding along the road I noticed a red snow fence. I didn't think much about it until I observed that, on the other side of the fence as I looked through the small slats, the grass was of a reddish color! I looked more intently and at the end of the fence I could see that the grass was real green, but behind the fence — red!

Did you ever watch the sun about to set in the West, when suddenly it began to rain? What did you say? I know — "there must be a rainbow."

Sure enough, there it was in all its beautiful colors. The rainbow is seen only through the rain.

Because of the glasses we have on or because of the red fence the grass appears to be red.

Yes, we sometimes misjudge people because of what we think about them. Maybe jealousy creeps up into our minds and we begin to "see red". But remember the red is in your own jealous thoughts — it has nothing to do with the other boy or girl at all. Tear down that "red fence."

Don't blame someone else for what YOU have done. I recall that Jesus once said to people who were always seeing evil in others:

"He that is without sin among you, let him first cast a stone at her." JOHN 8:7 READ PSALM 101.

A MESSAGE FROM OUR BIBLE

"I will sing of mercy and judgment; unto thee, O Lord will I sing.

I will behave myself wisely in a perfect way. —

He that worketh deceit shall not dwell within my house; he that telleth lies shall not tarry in my sight.

I will early destroy all the wicked of the land; that I may cut off all wicked doers from the city of the Lord." — PSALM 101:1-2, 7-8.

LET US PRAY

Dear Lord, — Teach us how to pray. Help us to feel thy presence around about us at all times. Let us not be too hasty in accusing others of wrong until we examine our own faults.

Grant that we may so live as to encourage people who feel downhearted and discouraged. Give us strength and generosity that we may want to give aid to those in need.

Bless thy Church, O God, and make us a real helpful part of it, and keep us ever faithful to the ideas and ideals for which it stands.

Give us willing minds and hearts that we may send help to children all over the world who need what we can give. **AMEN.**

—SOUNDS YOU CANNOT HEAR—

Science books tell us that there are many sounds which nobody can hear. Many insects talk beyond the range of the human ear.

You can see sound sometimes, when you can't hear it. Put some tiny iron filings on a piece of paper, then hold a magnet beneath the paper, and as you move it back and forth watch the particles of iron filings hit together and form various patterns. Can you hear them hit each other? No!

There are sounds you can't hear but which you can feel, — when the church organ is playing do you sometimes feel the pew actually vibrate just a little? It does happen, and the notes that make it vibrate are so low in the bass section that you can't hear them.

You never heard a bat sing; in fact, the voices of many insects are too shrill to be heard by human ears. But these all seem to be able to hear us! Any slight sound we make seems to startle them.

Isn't our relationship to God in prayer something like that? He hears our prayers whether we speak in words, or silently think them, and He answers, we may be sure of that!

He answers, not to our ears but He truly speaks to your conscience and mine, disturbing us, telling us what is right and what is wrong.

He surely speaks to our hearts and minds, telling us clearly that love is better than hate. That we should be kind and considerate toward one another, and always trustworthy. Thus did Jesus grow, not only physically, but also mentally and spiritually, — *"In favor with God and man."* — LUKE 2:52.

A MESSAGE FROM OUR BIBLE

"Lord, now lettest thou thy servant depart in peace, according to thy word;
For mine eyes have seen thy salvation.
Which thou hast prepared before the face of all people;
A light to lighten the Gentiles, and the glory of thy people Israel.
And the child grew, and waxed strong in spirit, filled with wisdom; and the grace of God was upon him.
And Jesus increased in wisdom, and stature, and in favour with God and man." — LUKE 2:29-32, 40, 52.

LET US PRAY

Dear God, — As Jesus became strong he used his strength for others. Physically he was able to walk great distances to help someone. Mentally he understood thy purpose for him and spiritually he developed in kindness and love. Grant that we, like Him, may truly and wisely serve thee, in Jesus' name. AMEN.

IN EVERYTHING, THERE IS MUSIC

A long time ago I was attending a very nice concert with orchestral as well as singing parts. It was rather an ornate affair with guest soloists and an outstanding leader.

This orchestra director could take any of the instruments and play it so professionally and smoothly. He brought forth beautiful music from each one.

Then a little fun came on the scene. A man in coveralls came in with a saw and started to saw a protruding board from the entrance doorway.

Of course this stopped the music program and the director looked very angry. He rushed over to the workman and grabbed the saw from him, and was about to throw it away when he reached over and took a bow from one of the violinists — placed the end of the saw between his knees — bent it over, and drew the bow across it. The audience was raptured and began to burst out in applause when they heard the beautiful rendition of strains from a familiar musical number. He was kept playing the saw for many minutes!

It would seem that this master could produce music from anything!

Indeed there is music and beauty in everything at the Master's touch. Even in you and in me.

Jesus is the master and if we would all put ourselves in his hands and under his guidance, this would be a happier world, and it would be filled with the music and harmony of peace and love.

In everything and everyone there is music when in the hands of the master.

"As he drew near to the house, he heard music." — LUKE 15:25.

A MESSAGE FROM OUR BIBLE

"But the father said to his servants, Bring forth the best robe, and put it on him; and put a ring on his hand, and shoes on his feet;

And bring hither the fatted calf, and kill it; and let us eat, and be merry;

For this my son was dead, and is alive again; he was lost, and is found. And they began to be merry.

"It was meet that we should make merry, and be glad; for this thy brother was dead. and is alive again; and was lost and is found." — LUKE 15:22-25, 32.

LET US PRAY

Dear Lord, we thank thee for happiness, the kind that gives more than it receives. As Jesus found true joy in service, help us to have the willingness to serve and the desire to be kind, that we may find complete happiness in the love of Jesus Christ. AMEN.

WHEELBARROWS

The dictionary says that a wheelbarrow has "one wheel and two handles." It has a box-like body in which many things may be carried from one place to another.

A wheelbarrow has no motor attached to it, neither does it have any horsepower! It is operated by the hands of man.

There are three things involved in operating a wheelbarrow. If it is empty there is no difficulty whatever, but if it is loaded — let us say, — with six crates of oranges, it becomes quite a trick to wheel the load to its destination. First you have to *lift* — taking hold of the handles and having the load of oranges well balanced. You will find, if one hand has more lifting weight than the other, that the wheelbarrow may tip over and spill out the crates! Then another important effort must be made — you must *push*!

When Jesus came to the world he talked to the disciples and told them to take the love of God and his message, and carry it to all parts of the world. The church was organized and became the means by which God's message and love was carried.

But, as with the wheelbarrow, you and I must lift; and we must be well balanced ourselves, filled with Christian faith and love, and then push, eagerly anxious to give the gospel to all around us.

"*They . . . spread abroad his fame in all that country.*"
— MATTHEW 9:31.

A MESSAGE FROM OUR BIBLE

"And when he was come into the house, the blind men came to Him; and Jesus said unto them, Believe ye that I am able to do this? They said unto him, yea, Lord.

Then touched he their eyes saying. According to your faith be it unto you.

And their eyes were opened; and Jesus straitly charged them, saying, See that no man know it.

But they, when they were departed, spread abroad his fame in all that country." — MATTHEW 9:28-31.

LET US PRAY

Our Father in Heaven, — we thank thee for so arranging our world that there are opportunities for us all to help make it a better place. Bless our homes and grant that each one may do his best to keep them happy. In this way we spread thy Gospel of truth and love to many around us.

With thankful hearts we would express thy will in Jesus' Name. AMEN.

YOUR WEIGHT

Have you noticed that in subway stations and in many public places there are one or two of those penny weighing machines? and very often someone is standing on one of them! People seem to like to be weighed.

Your weight is what you can balance, without using any outside pressure like someone putting his foot on the scales!

The weight of your muscles is designated by how much you can lift! How much work you can do.

It seems to me that the true weight of a dollar bill should be, how much it can buy.

You have a heart. I don't think it has ever been weighed on one of those penny scales! But I believe God weighs it by the amount of kindness and love it can balance. Being big-hearted or light-hearted does not refer to scales.

What is the weight of your voice? You have heard people say, "what he says carries a lot of weight." Of course the meaning is that he is very influential and people heed and obey his counsel. The words of Jesus, indeed his whole life, were like that. Jesus' life can only be weighed by the love and service that he gives to the world.

Your true weight is measured not only in terms of pounds and ounces but much more it is measured by service and character and your influence for good.

"Let me be weighed in an even balance." — JOB 31:6.

A MESSAGE FROM OUR BIBLE

"Wherewithal shall a young man cleanse his way? by taking heed according to thy word.

With my whole heart have I sought thee; O let me not wander from thy commandments.

Thy word have I hid in my heart, that I might not sin against thee.

Blessed art thou, O Lord; teach me thy statutes.

I will delight myself in thy statutes; I will not forget thy word." — PSALM 119:9-12, 16.

LET US PRAY

Dear God, Our Father, — We thank thee for the assurance of thy patience with us. We act so terribly sometimes, but we are sorry, and as thou dost forgive us, help us to do better and to be better each day.

Bless our homes, dear Lord, and keep us patient with those around us, and forgiving, that in thy sight we may be growing to be more like Jesus. AMEN.

A CANDLE

One of the most beautiful of church worship programs is a Candlelight Service when many candles are lighted from a single one which is usually on the altar table.

This, of course, inspires us to catch the spirit of God's love by the example of Jesus Christ who was the Light from His Father to give us light.

So a candle, to be a light, must first be lighted. The candle is not a light until it is touched by a light. It does not light itself but it is always ready to be lighted!

When a candle is once lighted it will stay lighted until something like a draft extinguishes it. It does not extinguish itself unless it is placed in a box without oxygen!

The purpose of a lighted candle is to extinguish darkness and that is exactly what it does, — but if all the black darkness in the whole world were crowded into one small room, it could not extinguish that little light of the candle!

When Jesus came as the Light of the world, wicked men tried to do away with him, but even though they crucified him, they could never destroy his influence. All these years his love has been an ever-lasting bright spot slowly driving out the darkness of sin and evil, hate and greed.

As we accept the light of God's truth from Jesus, we help disperse the darkness of wrong, even as the sun drives out the night!

"——— *walk in the light* ———" I JOHN 1:7.

A MESSAGE FROM OUR BIBLE

"This then is the message which we have heard of him, and declare unto you, that God is light, and in him is no darkness at all.

If we say that we have fellowship with him, and walk in darkness, we lie, and do not the truth;

But if we walk in the light, as he is in the light, we have fellowship one with another, and the blood of Jesus Christ his Son cleanseth us from all sin." I JOHN 1:5-7.

LET US PRAY

Dear Father in Heaven, — we thank thee for Jesus, who came and taught us to understand thy love for us.

Help us to be more like Him as opportunities come to us to show unselfishness. As a light makes clear and safe the road ahead, so may we be an example to show others the right way of life.

Bless our homes, dear Lord, and protect us in thy care, we ask. AMEN.

THANK YOU, GOD

When we pray we don't need to say a lot of high-sounding big words. He knows how intelligent we are without telling Him! He just wants us to be good and kind and appreciative toward each other and He knows we will be if we are thoughtful and worshipful toward Him.

So, many times a day, let us each say "thank you" to God, telling Him how much we love and need Him and appreciate His many gifts and opportunities.

In 1621 — over three hundred years ago — Governor Bradford proclaimed "a Thanksgiving unto God for the plenteous harvest." So after a church service with a long sermon, they gathered, not only just their little group, but with the friendly Indians, for a dinner, — a sort of love feast. Beginning in 1680, this became an annual event in New England.

Nearly two hundred years later Mrs. Sarah Hale of Philadelphia and of New England heritage, thought that the whole country should set aside a day of Thanksgiving to God, so she wrote to the several State governors, and finally to President Lincoln, who appointed the last Thursday of November 1864 as national Thanksgiving Day, and each President, since, has followed his example, with only a "slight variation of the day."

God has supplied us with so many blessings it is impossible to name them all! He doesn't expect us to; however, He does want us to talk with Him and show Him how happy we are, and we certainly should, often, say "thank you, God" even if we say no more. If we truly mean it and say it often, God is pleased with our prayers.

"After this manner pray, our Father———." — MATTHEW 6:9.

A MESSAGE FROM OUR BIBLE

"But when you pray use not vain repetitions, as the heathen do; for they think that they shall be heard for their much speaking.

Be not ye therefore like unto them; for your Father knoweth what things ye have need of, before ye ask him.

After this manner therefore pray ye: Our Father which art in heaven, Hallowed be thy name.

Thy kingdom come. Thy will be done in earth, as it is in heaven.

Give us this day our daily bread.

And forgive us our debts, as we forgive our debtors.

And lead us not into temptation, but deliver us from evil; For thine is the kingdom, and the power, and the glory, forever. Amen." — MATTHEW 6:7-13.

LET US PRAY

We thank thee, dear God, for Jesus whom thou didst send to us as an example of actions and words. Help us to be more like him in our every day living.

We thank thee for the many opportunities we have for being thoughtful and kind. When we are urged to do wrong or speak evil, thoughts of him are present to check us. We do thank thee, God, for thy watchful care. AMEN.

IVY

Some time ago I saw a very lovely brick church with a towering steeple rising from the roof. The thing that attracted my attention particularly was the fact that the building was almost completely covered with ivy.

I decided to see if I could play the part of "Jack" of the beanstalk. So I chose my stalk of ivy and climbed up and up and up — in imagination — until I was at the end of it, and found myself part way up on the steeple!

Ivy has the tendency to climb upward because it seeks the light that comes from above. Mrs. Sargent once had an ivy growing on a large spinning wheel. Spoke by spoke it was trained as it grew upward until the wheel was covered. All the leaves, however, were toward the light, that came through the window, so it was most beautiful from the outside!

Ivy never likes to grow downward. It has an upward look, eager to climb.

Ivy is different, too, from most plants, — it depends on something upon which to grow, and, attaching itself to it, beautifies the object it associates with.

Are your friends happy when you are with them? Is your home happier because of you? Jesus spread happiness and joy wherever he went because his thoughts were always upward towards God, the source of spiritual light.

A Christian is like the ivy, stretching out to the sides, trying to be useful and helpful to people, but always reaching upward toward the source of light, toward God.

"He who does what is true, comes to the light." — JOHN 3:21.

A MESSAGE FROM OUR BIBLE

"For God so loved the world, that he gave his only begotten Son, that whosoever believeth in him should not perish, but have everlasting life.

For God sent not his Son into the world to condemn the world; but that the world through him might be saved.

Everyone that doeth evil hateth the light, neither cometh to the light, lest his deeds should be reproved.

But he that doeth truth cometh to the light, that his deeds may be made manifest, that they are wrought in God." — JOHN 3:16-17, 20-21.

LET US PRAY

Dear Lord — Help me to live the kind of life thou would like me to live. I thank thee for thy words, which I read in the Bible, that tell me to speak kindly of others. Thou hast taught me to pray and it gives me courage when I am afraid. It gives me strength when I am weak.

Guide me, O God, in the way of truth and help me always, to be trustworthy. In Jesus' name, AMEN.

HOW BIRDS FLY

It was snowing. The first storm of the winter. The birds were taken unaware and I saw one fall onto the ground in about two inches of snow. He just couldn't "take off." He couldn't run fast enough in that snow to jump and get high enough to use his wings. You see, birds fly by using their wings, and when, with a little help, my bird got into the air, he flew far far away!

Airplanes are much like that bird — as long as their wings keep them in the air they glide along beautifully and safely to their destination; but if they get tired and come down into the snow in some mountain side, they just give up until they are helped off the ground.

Did you ever start something like knitting a sweater or playing the piano and then suddenly drop it for some other interest? I guess we all have. How difficult it is later to start over again where you left off!

You see birds fly by flying, by using their wings. If an eagle should refuse to use his wings for a year — or even a few months — he would have difficulty in starting to fly again. It seems to me there is a pretty good idea there for all of us.

When you start something, keep at it! Don't give up just because you are tired or because you want to do something else — finish what you start to do and then "pick up" after you; put your playthings away in their proper places.

The Sunday School is where you learn to live on a high level with Jesus. Remembering that birds fly by flying so you show yourself a Christian by doing Christian acts, by speaking kind words, by living every day with thoughts of Jesus leading you forward on a high level and keeping you up there, and at making the following words your promise to Jesus:

"I will follow thee, Lord —" LUKE 9:61.

A MESSAGE FROM OUR BIBLE

"And behold a certain lawyer stood up, and tempted him, saying, Master what shall I do to inherit eternal life?

And he answering said, Thou shalt love the Lord thy God with all thy heart, and with all thy soul, and with all thy strength, and with all thy mind; and thy neighbour as thyself.

And he said unto him, Thou hast answered right, this do, and thou shalt live." LUKE 10: 25, 27-28.

LET US PRAY

Our Father in heaven — we thank thee for the words thou hast spoken to us through the men who wrote our Bible. Thou dost speak to each one of us as long as we listen to hear.

Grant that our thoughts may be lofty, and that we may follow thee in thy great teachings. Help us drive out those things from our thoughts that are wrong. Give us peace and love, and bless our homes. In Christ's name we ask. AMEN.

KEY LOGS

Many many years ago, during the winter months, woodsmen would go into the north country in the Connecticut and Ammonoosuc valleys and chop down trees, and saw them into great logs.

Then, in the Spring after the ice had broken up and melted out of the rivers leaving them to nearly overflowing their banks, these millions of logs would be rolled into the great streams, and down the rivers they would come, perhaps as far as one hundred miles to saw mills.

Sometimes just out in front of our house there would come a thunderous boom. I knew at once it was blasting, so I would run out, and sure enough, there was a great log jam in the river. Millions of logs were piled up four and six, perhaps twenty deep, and they were holding back logs as far as I could see!

Men with hobnail boots were running around over those logs, with the river rushing along under them, looking for a Key log.

One log got caught on a rock and it stopped another and another until finally no logs could pass down the river — and the force of the current piled them on top of each other.

Finally the key log was found and blasted loose, and all the others began to move!

You boys and girls have chosen to be Christians. I hope not a single one of you will ever be snagged on some rock of temptation or habit.

It makes me sad when I see a young boy caught and mastered by a cigarette or just some hateful disposition, because I'm afraid he will influence some other boy to bad habits that are cheap and dirty.

Keep yourself clean and respected, and you won't hurt other people. You see one log can cause a jam, so one bad habit leads to another and makes for sadness and hardship among a lot of people.

Keep yourself 'unspotted from the world.' JAMES 1:27.

A MESSAGE FROM OUR BIBLE

"Wherefore, my beloved brethren, let every man be swift to hear, slow to speak, slow to wrath;

For the wrath of man worketh not the righteousness of God.

If any man among you seem to be religious, and bridleth not his tongue, but deceiveth his own heart, this man's religion is vain.

Pure religion and undefiled before God and the Father is this, To visit the fatherless and the widows in their affliction, and to keep himself unspotted from the world."
JAMES 1:19-20, 26-27.

LET US PRAY

Our Father in Heaven — We thank thee for thy love toward us. We thank thee for thy Son Jesus, who lived and died that we might know the extent of thy love.

Speak to our hearts, O Lord, and show us how to be more like Jesus as He kept Himself unspotted from the world.

Watch over us, we ask, and keep us from wrong acts, and from speaking evil words, and so develop within us peaceful minds. AMEN.

"BICYCLES"

When you go out to the garage — or to the street and step into your automobile you find it a very simple procedure. You just open the door and sit down and wait for the car to start.

It's the same with an airplane. Even a horse will stand still and let you mount without much maneuvering.

But a bicycle! Of course you can lean it against a fence or a tree and have little trouble getting on it. But that is not the way to do it!

You have to LEARN to get on to a bicycle. It is almost like trying to mount a colt that has never been ridden.

What fun for those who watch you! What bruises you get trying to master that thing! Learning to ride a bicycle.

A bicycle has to be moving when you get aboard, otherwise you are right off again, flat on your face with your feet tangled in the wheels and the saddle on top of you! The second you are on — even before you actually get seated, you have to start pedaling — and then the faster you pedal the surer you are of staying on.

In fact it is very simple to ride a bicycle when you are going fast, and actually it is much safer — except in the street or sidewalk when you might hit someone who is walking.

You see, actually, a bicycle is of little use unless it is going somewhere, unless it is active.

If you stop and think about it, the bicycle has a good lesson for you. God gave you hands and feet, not to be idle or to be harmful in any way to others, but to be active and to have a purpose — to so live that others will find happiness because of you and may be led into right ways of service.

Jesus taught us all that kind of leadership, when, according to a statement by Paul:

"He went about doing good." ACTS 10:38.

A MESSAGE FROM OUR BIBLE

"God anointed Jesus of Nazareth with the Holy Spirit and with power; who went about doing good, and healing all that were oppressed for God was with him.

And we are witnesses of all things which he did both in the land of the Jews, and in Jerusalem; whom they slew and hanged on a tree.

Him God raised up the third day, and shewed him openly." THE ACTS 10:38-40.

LET US PRAY

We thank thee, dear Lord, for our Church and the thoughtful and kindly spirit of Christian people.

We thank thee for the sacrificial spirit of generosity as declared by thy Son Jesus, who showed the real depth of his love and loyalty as he went about doing thy will. He helped others and even died that we all might be saved from selfishness to usefulness, from greediness to sharing.

Let thy power, through us, strengthen the weak and guide the ignorant and lead all to the knowledge of thee. AMEN.

TAPE RECORDING

"Boys flying kites haul in their white-winged birds. But you can't do that way when you're flying words."

I have quoted that couplet before, many times. How true it is. Once you have said something and a person has heard your words, they become fixed in his mind and it is difficult, yes, almost impossible for him to erase them!

But I believe they *can* be erased, — forgotten.

It is quite a hobby now, among some people to set up a tape recording outfit in a room and record all the conversation, unknown to those present! After playing the record back several times, to the delight of some, and the embarrassment of others, done, of course, all in fun, — the tape is cleared of all words and it can be used again.

I hope no one ever says anything mean and untrue to you, but if someone does, do you hold it in your memory and bring it out and talk about it now and then? — or do you just put it to one side and forget it? Of course it is easier to forget if the person says "I'm sorry."

You see—words impressed on tape can easily be erased, but it is much more difficult to erase spoken words from the mind and memory of the person who hears them. It can be done! If you speak words that are unkind, just say you are sorry, and then say some nice words to take their place.

Consider God before you speak, that you may be proud to have your words reproduced as recorded.

"Let the words of my mouth . . . . be acceptable in thy sight, O Lord." PSALM 19:14.

A MESSAGE FROM OUR BIBLE

"The heavens declare the glory of God and the firmament showeth his handywork.

Day unto day uttereth speech, and night unto night showeth knowledge.

There is no speech nor language where their voice is not heard.

Their line is gone out through all the earth, and their words to the end of the world. In them hath he set a tabernacle for the sun.

Let the words of my mouth, and the meditation of my heart, be acceptable in thy sight, O Lord, my strength and my redeemer." THE PSALMS 19:1-4, 14.

LET US PRAY

Dear God, — We thank thee for Jesus, and the words of counsel he has given us, as recorded in our Bible. His messages are as true and important today as the day they were spoken.

Help us to heed his words of wisdom and grant that we may repeat them often to others that they, too, may profit by them.

Grant that we may always speak kindly, that thy love may be reproduced through us. AMEN.

HORNETS

Have you a dime in your pocket? Look at it. You will see there a bundle of sticks. If you count them you will find there are forty-eight. Of course two more will have to be added this year (1960), because each stick represents a State.

These are not just separated sticks, but forty-eight tied together.

Our fifty States are united in bonds of law and order. Each will help the others to be strong.

One toothpick can easily be broken, — but when fifty are bound together it is difficult to break them.

I'm reminded of the man who had a lash whip. He said he could hit a hornet sitting on a tree limb, but when he was asked to hit a nest of hornets he said — "No sir! They are organized!"

As a Christian boy or girl you can do a lot to help some one else to obey God and to speak truth as Jesus would do. But when you join forces with hundreds of other people in an organized Church, many people — even a whole nation will be influenced by your message and service.

So be loyal to your church and work hard in it that it may be strong and influential in its organized service for Christ.

One boy can't win a ball game but nine can if they work together. When those fishermen came in from Lake Galilee without any fish Jesus told them to go out and try again. This time their nets were full "yet the net was not broken." Although the net seems frail with its small strings, it is strong because the strings are bound together. JOHN 21:11.

A MESSAGE FROM OUR BIBLE

"Simon Peter said unto them, I go a fishing. They say unto him, We also go with thee. They went forth, and entered into a ship immediately; and that night they caught nothing.

And Jesus said unto them, Cast the net on the right side of the ship, and ye shall find. They cast, therefore, and now they were not able to draw it for the multitude of fishes.

Simon Peter went up, and drew the net to land full of great fishes, an hundred and fifty and three; and for all there were so many, yet was not the net broken." JOHN 21:3, 6, 11.

LET US PRAY

O God, our Father — We thank thee for the daily opportunities that present themselves for our solution. Give us strength to catch hold of the many opportunities that come near us each day and hour.

We thank thee for fellowship that helps to bind all people together, that we may grow in peace among the nations.

Give us the strength, through our church, to carry thy Gospel of truth to all who would deny thee, or through indifference and self-interest would by-pass thee and thy will.

Accept us, and our abilities, and use us in thy great plan of righteousness. AMEN.

MODELS

When I look at the cover of the Saturday Evening Post and see a boy some artist has drawn I immediately wonder who the model was who sat for the painting. Whom did the artist look at as the pattern for his picture?

I have often stood looking at the Statue of Liberty situated just outside of New York City. It stands there as a great symbol of welcome, security, enlightenment and love.

Who but a mother could have been the model?

So I looked up the history of this Statue and sure enough — the model was the Sculptor's own mother, Charlotte B. Bartholdi.

When I look at a boy or girl I often wonder whose example makes him speak and act the way he does. What hero of that child developed within him such a clean, fine lad. Some day when you grow a little older you may be a hero or an example for some small boy or girl to copy.

If we seriously want this world to really be a safe and happy place you boys and girls just take Jesus as your model, and try to live like Him. In all you do and say, take a good look at Jesus before you speak. Be a living symbol of honor and christian love.

Let Jesus be your model and you, in turn, will be an "example" for others.

PHILIPPIANS 3:17.

A MESSAGE FROM OUR BIBLE

"I press toward the mark for the prize of the high calling of God in Christ Jesus.

Be followers together of me, and mark them which walk so as ye have us for an ensample.

For our conversation is in heaven; from whence also we look for the Saviour, the Lord Jesus Christ;

Who shall change our vile body, that it may be fashioned like unto his glorious body according to the working whereby he is able even to subdue all things unto himself."
PHILIPPIANS 3:14, 17, 20-21.

LET US PRAY

Dear God, Our Father, — Help us to see the right, when we have to choose between two or more ways of action.

Show us the right way, dear Lord, and give us the strength of courage to stand by it.

Help us to keep our conversation clean so that the example we set may lead others in the right path. Teach us the love and kindness that was in thy heart, that we may express it in our own actions towards each other, — In thy name we ask. AMEN.

KEEP WALKING

Did you ever stand in the sunshine and try to dodge your shadow? No matter how fast you would jump back and forth or from side to side your shadow jumped with you! The only way for you to dodge your shadow is to stand still. Gradually, almost unseen, your shadow will move. Actually it will dodge you!

Furthermore, if you stand still in one place all day the shadow will go away. Even if you stand near a house and don't move for a few hours your shadow will leave.

In order to be sure to cast a shadow all day you have to keep walking. Jesus put it this way: "Walk in the light". (see John 8:12). Follow Jesus and walk in the light.

Do you ever get out of bed in the morning and feel out of sorts, — wishing you didn't have to go to school? Some older people are like that too at times. Just walk out into the bright sunshine and thank God for a new day. Stop for a minute or two before you eat your breakfast and thank God for food.

Quietly thank God for your home and parents and, yes, your teachers. Start the day by walking with God in the light of his love and care. Don't stay grumpy and disagreeable, letting the light of joy and happiness get away from you. Walk along with God all day and let His love and goodness shed its light upon you and you won't see your shadow for it will be behind you — if you keep walking in the right direction.

"Walk ye in Him." COLOSSIANS 2:6.

A MESSAGE FROM OUR BIBLE

"For though I be absent in the flesh, yet am I with you in the spirit, joying and beholding your order, and the steadfastness of your faith in Christ.

As ye have therefore received Christ Jesus the Lord so walk ye in him:

Rooted and built up in Him, and established in the faith, as ye have been taught, abounding therein with thanksgiving." COLOSSIANS 2:5-7.

LET US PRAY

Dear God, Our Father — We thank thee for all thy beautiful things in the world. These many things show us how much thou dost love us. Make us thoughtful that we too may express love and kindness, that children around us may be happy.

Teach us how to walk with thee and so become more and more like Jesus, who dedicated himself to help all people to see and understand thy love. AMEN.

SCREENS

I wonder if you know what a filter is? Perhaps you have seen one on the cold water faucet at the kitchen sink! It is a kind of screen to catch the dirt particles (and tiny bugs) that sometimes come through the water pipes, so that the water will be pure to drink.

We put screens in our windows during the summer time to keep out the flies and mosquitoes.

When your mother wants to sift some flour into the milk while she is making a cake, so there will be no lumps, she uses a kind of screen, so that only the nice fine flour goes through.

Sometimes the sugar becomes caked into small lumps. Mother puts it into a sieve or screen, and shakes the sugar so as to break the lumps. Those that are too hard, remain in the sieve to be used for other purposes.

Almost every day you have to make a decision. You have to choose between two things you want to do. Or perhaps you have to make a choice between right and wrong. How nice it would be if you only had a screen that would keep out the bad and leave you the only right choice.

I find that a prayer, asking what Jesus would do, helps a great deal in causing me to make the right decision. Prayer serves as a screen, shutting out of our lives that which is evil or untrue.

"Abhor that which is evil, cleave to what is good." — ROMANS 12:9.

A MESSAGE FROM OUR BIBLE

"Let love be without dissimulation. Abhor that which is evil; cleave to that which is good.

Be kindly affectioned one to another with brotherly love; in honor preferring one another;

Not slothful in business; fervent in spirit; serving the Lord.

Rejoicing in hope; patient in tribulation; continuing instant in prayer." ROMANS 12:9-12.

LET US PRAY

Father in Heaven, teach us to pray — As thy love was expressed in Jesus, give us the ability to show it in our every day play with other children.

Keep us from being selfish or irritable and make us thoughtful of others, and considerate.

Bless all children who need help, and give us helpful and generous minds.

Help us to be serious in our intentions that we may truly serve thee unselfishly in all we do and say. AMEN.

AUXANOMETERS

If you should go to a store and ask for a yard of ribbon, the clerk would measure it out with a yard stick. An acre of land would be measured in rods. A piece of steak would be apportioned to you by weight. How tall are you? Five feet and one inch, you may say.

We once had, in front of our house, a very interesting bush. It died every Fall so that I took the stalks away; but every Spring it began to grow from its roots. I could almost see it grow! This kind of bamboo bush grew as much as five inches in a single night until it reached about eight feet high. To measure its growth I would use an Auxanometer which a dictionary told me "measures the growth of plants."

So it seems that everything can be measured for height, or depth, or growth or value.

In thinking about this hard-to-pronounce word I began to wonder how you and I can be measured for value. Just what are you good for and how much?

In measuring, one thing is compared with something else. So it is, we compare ourselves with others. And it seems to me, as Christians we are measured by the life of Jesus. Indeed I would like to coin a word — "Christonometer": to measure the value of a person.

"According to the measure of the rule which God hath distributed to us." — 2 CORINTHIANS 10:13.

A MESSAGE FROM OUR BIBLE

"We will not boast of things without our measure, but according to the measure of the rule which God hath distributed to us, a measure to reach even unto you.

For we stretch not ourselves beyond our measure, as though we reached not unto you; for we are come as far as to you also in preaching the gospel of Christ; —

He that glorieth, let him glory in the Lord.

For not he that commendeth himself is approved, but whom the Lord commendeth." — 2 CORINTHIANS 10:13, 14, 17-18.

LET US PRAY

Dear Jesus, — We thank thee for happy days. For our homes and for oMther and Dad who love us, and whom we love. Help us to show that love by thinking of their wishes when we are asked to do something for them. Make us ready to respond without being grumpy and selfish. May thy way, not ours be done until our way becomes thy way.

So help us to be good, and teach us to do right, and lead us to be thoughtful as we play with other children. Watch over us, we pray, especially all who are unhappy. AMEN.

"DON'T LOWER YOUR THROWING ARM"

I once heard Roy Campanella, one of the greatest catchers in baseball, say: "Don't lower your throwing arm." What he meant by this statement was that the second a catcher catches the ball he should keep his arm in readiness to throw to second base — or to any other player.

If he lowers his arm as the ball hits the mitt, then he must raise it just so much farther before he can throw. Try it sometime and you will understand better what he meant when he said "Don't lower your throwing arm."

It is almost like putting off until tomorrow something you ought to do today.

Haven't you been going to the store for some eggs and you remember your mother saying, — "Now go right along and come right back. I want an egg for this cake. It's all ready but that, so hurry." You hurry out of the house all right and start running up the street. Suddenly you see two dogs fighting; several boys are watching so you join them. Ten minutes, and a yelping dog later, you remember the errand, — and when you finally get home you have to stay in the house for one hour! I don't need to tell you why! You see you "lowered your throwing arm" and lost the game! You dawdled on the way, forgot the eggs for a time; the cake was spoiled and you got punished.

You may say that the dog fight was worth the punishment, but that is not the point. The point is that *you* failed and the cake was a failure BECAUSE of you.

Keep yourself trustworthy and always ready — don't lower your throwing arm.

"They that were ready went in." — MATTHEW 25:10.

A MESSAGE FROM OUR BIBLE

"Then shall the kingdom of heaven be likened unto ten virgins, which took their lamps, and went forth to meet the bridegroom.

And at midnight there was a cry made, Behold the bridegroom cometh; go ye out to meet him.

Then all those virgins arose and trimmed their lamps.

And the foolish said unto the wise, Give us of your oil; for our lamps are gone out.

But the wise answered, saying, Not so; lest there be not enough for us and you; but go ye rather to them that sell, and buy for yourselves.

And while they went to buy, the bridegroom came; and they that were ready went in with him to the marriage; and the door was shut." — MATTHEW 25 : 1, 6-10.

LET US PRAY

Our Father in Heaven, — Teach us to pray as Jesus did, not with ourselves in mind but thinking of others' needs. Grant that we may be helpful in making thy love live in their midst.

We see thy love expressed in the beauty of growing things around us, and we know thou dost love us more.

Help us to always be faithful in our every day relationship with thee and with one another, and may we so live as to give joy to all around us. We seek thy help in what we do. AMEN.

BY YOUR WEIGHT

There is an expression which sometimes describes a person who seems to have a lot of influence upon many people: "He likes to throw his weight around."

I thought of that statement when I was riding on a bus not long ago. I wanted to get off so I rang the buzzer — the bus stopped. I went to the door and waited for it to open, but it didn't, I was just about to call to the operator when someone said "step down." Sure enough, when I stepped down onto the first step the door opened! My weight made an electric contact which, in turn, threw open the door.

When you see things you ought to do, do you always step right up and get at it? Or do you wait for someone else to "open the door" for you?

When you see a piece of paper fluttering around on the street, and there is a waste can near, do you step right down from the sidewalk and pick it up so that your street will look better? Or do you let it go and complain of the lack of street cleaners to "pick up."

In the winter there is snow to shovel sometimes. I hope you step right down with all your weight and clean the sidewalk carefully, and don't think you have to wait for someone to offer you a dollar or two for the little task. I've seen boys shoulder shovels and start out seeking to shovel peoples' driveways — while right at home their mothers are clearing their own walks, and then when Dad comes home from work he has his driveway to shovel!

Don't "throw your weight around" until you are sure you are unselfish in what you do.

"All the doors were opened." — THE ACTS 16:26.

A MESSAGE FROM OUR BIBLE

"And at midnight Paul and Silas prayed, and sang praises unto God; and the prisoners heard them.

And suddenly there was a great earthquake, so that the foundations of the prison were shaken; and immediately all the doors were opened and every one's bands were loosed.

And the keeper of the prison awaking out of his sleep, and seeing the prison doors open, he drew his sword, and would have killed himself, supposing that the prisoners had been fled.

But Paul cried with a loud voice saying, "Do thyself no harm: for we are all here." — THE ACTS 16:25-28.

LET US PRAY

Dear God, — Please give us a forgiving spirit. We dislike to be angry, so teach us to overcome such feelings when they come to us. If others seem to hurt us help us to remember that we may be partly to blame.

Grant that we may be trustworthy in thy sight and be always ready to obey thy council as revealed to us by the life of Jesus.

We ask thee to bless our homes and our church, and may we, through the church, convey thy message to the whole world and may all come to serve thee in Christ's name. AMEN.

CHARGE IT

This parable has nothing to do with buying something at a store without leaving any money to pay for it.

I like to watch a ball game on television sometimes, and the thing that impresses me most seems to be the alertness of every player. In fact the pitcher, before he delivers a ball, turns and looks at the other eight men. Are they in position? Are they alert or are they talking to each other or hunting for four leaf clovers!

It seems to me that two of the nine men are most alert, ready for anything — a strike, a hit, or fly or a roller. These two men are the Catcher and the Shortstop, and of the two, the shortstop seems the most active.

The Shortstop is not too far from the batter and, like the pitcher, he is the most liable to get hurt when a hard hit ball comes bullet-like right at him.

So alert is the shortstop that when a ground ball is hit his way he charges it! He doesn't wait for the ball to come to him, he instantly rushes towards it, thereby saving a second or two in throwing the ball to first for a put-out.

For a shortstop to charge the ball, often makes the difference between winning or losing the game, and maybe the series.

When you know you have a little duty to perform, do you say "Oh dear" or "I hate to think about it"; do you ask mother if you can put it off until night, or tomorrow morning? "I'll get up early and do my studying", — or do you *charge it*, and get it done and out of the way so you will be ready for a good mark.

"Therefore be ye also ready." — MATTHEW 24:44.

A MESSAGE FROM OUR BIBLE

"Watch therefore; for ye know not what hour your Lord doth come.

But know this, that if the goodman of the house had known in what watch the thief would come, he would have watched, and would not have suffered his house to be broken up.

Therefore be ye also ready; for in such an hour as ye think not the Son of man cometh." — MATTHEW 24:42-44.

LET US PRAY

Dear Lord, — If we have done or said things today that have hurt someone, guide us to seek their forgiveness by making everything right before we go to bed tonight. We know that thou art forgiving, — make us forgiving too.

Help us always to be ready to use every opportunity that comes to us which will lead us to understand thy love as expressed in Jesus Christ. Help us to be strong enough to resist all wrong doing and lead us in the path of right. AMEN.

PULL OR KICK

When I was a boy back on the farm in Bath, New Hampshire there was one horse I liked to drive because he was fast; but he also was "ornery" or contrary, — hard to manage.

Before going into the stall beside him I had to speak sharply to him. He had a tendency to lift his hind leg and swing it back! But a sharp voice would usually quiet him, if it didn't I had other means of doing it, therefore he never really kicked me, but I always thought he would like to! And that was close enough!

Old Harry not only could travel fast, he could work hard. If he had a heavy load to pull he would dig right in and plant his feet down and that load would move. He was strong.

One thing I noticed about Harry, when he was pulling hard to move a load of hay or sand he never kicked. Indeed, he could not pull and kick at the same time!

I have noticed that children, when they are asked to do an errand or anything that is hard and distasteful to do, like studying sometimes, they put it off and argue about it — "Just a minute" or "Can't I wait until after supper?" or "Just wait until this program is over." But when they finally get down to work and start doing the errand or the task they know must be done, they are pretty quiet, and when they have finished they feel better and are usually happy.

So, whatever has to be done, get with it and start pulling and you won't do so much fussing about it — indeed you might like it, for every task is a challenge to your disposition. When you are "pulling" you usually are not "kicking" — and by the same rule: when you are kicking you probably are not pulling very hard.

"Be diligent that ye may be found of him in peace." — 2 PETER 3:14.

A MESSAGE FROM OUR BIBLE

"The Lord is not slack concerning his promise, as some men count slackness; but is long-suffering to us-ward, not willing that any should perish, but that all should come to repentance.

Wherefore, beloved, seeing that ye look for such things, be diligent that ye may be found of him in peace, without spot, and blameless.

And account that the long-suffering of our Lord is salvation. — 2 PETER 3:9, 14-15.

LET US PRAY

Dear God. — We thank thee for the Church, and for the leaders who have been faithful to thy commands. Give us the sense of true loyalty and make us diligent that what we do may influence others to know the way of Jesus. Even though we are not as strong nor as wise as those who teach, we believe thou dost have faith in us to grow as Jesus did to the knowledge and character of thy Son.

Help us, each one, to deserve thy blessing. AMEN.

A SMALL STONE

Did you ever try hurling a stone with a sling? It takes a lot of practice before you can be accurate. If the stone is too large it just won't go straight, it sort of rainbows and drops to the ground far short of the target.

The stone for your slingshot should be small and fairly smooth. You must keep your eyes on the target as you swing that little sling around and around —, you then let go of one end and follow through with your throwing arm.

You recall that boy David, when he said he would go out and meet Goliath, refused to take the armour and sword that were offered to him. They were all too heavy for him. All he wanted was his sling and five stones. He took five stones because he thought that, after he had finished with Goliath, his four sons might come forth for revenge, — but they all fled when they saw the power of little David who trusted God to help him destroy this giant ("Six cubits and a span") eleven feet, six and one half inches tall, and thus save his people from disaster.

Two things were very important in this incident — God and David. A great nation of people depended upon the ability of David, but David depended upon God. His great faith in God caused him to do his best, it caused him not to be afraid of Goliath, the giant, therefore he walked right up within sling shot distance of him while Goliath laughed at him.

That is good advice for all. If you have big or little troubles or problems or duties that you'd like to sidestep, — ask God to help you to step right up to them and see if they don't grow smaller, and become easier to handle.

"David chose five smooth stones." — 1 SAMUEL 17:40.

A MESSAGE FROM OUR BIBLE

"And Saul armed David with his armour and put a helmet of brass upon his head also he armed him with a coat of mail.

And David girded his sword upon his armour and he assayed to go; for he had not proved it. And David said unto Saul, I cannot go with these; for I have not proved them. And David put them off him.

And he took a staff in his hand and chose him five smooth stones, out of the brook and put them in a shepherd's bag which he had, even in a scrip; and his sling was in his hand; and he drew near to the Philistine." — 1 SAMUEL 17:38-40.

LET US PRAY

Our Father in Heaven, — We thank thee for every favor thou dost bestow upon us. We offer ourselves to thee, hoping we can be used to make this a better world. Though we are young, we have learned the meaning of right. We cannot do great things but thou didst use a small stone in the hands of a boy. Use us dear Lord, in some way.

Jesus has taught us to speak kindly and to be considerate of all people; may we always follow this teaching as our service. AMEN.

HELD BY A TONGUE

The Bible speaks about the tongue as being quite small, yet it is one of the most powerful parts of your body. Without it you can not talk — with it you often talk too much! Sometimes unkind words are spoken and someone is hurt deeply.

The tongue is a vital part of you. It is quite tender. If you bite it accidentally it hurts terribly for a few minutes.

I once saw a little girl running along the street past me on a very cold winter day. It was near zero. Suddenly she stopped at a store and looked in through the window in the door. I was going into that store, but just as I was about to push by her I saw that her tongue seemed to be lapping the little iron bar across the door window. She was crying. I knew she was caught. If she had pulled away it would have damaged her tongue. By breathing on the iron bar she was soon freed. She was rushed to the doctor and for several days her mouth was very full of a badly swollen tongue and it was a very painful experience.

Indeed your tongue can get you into a lot of trouble sometimes. The words it speaks not only hurt someone else but afterwards you are sorry you said them, and they hurt you too.

Don't ever let your tongue hurt you by allowing it to be caught on cold iron bars — or on evil or untruthful words. Take good care of your tongue, especially as to what it says. Let it always be considerate and in strict control.

"The tongue is a little member and boasteth great things." — JAMES 3:5.

A MESSAGE FROM OUR BIBLE

"If any man among you seem to be religious, and bridleth not his tongue, but deceiveth his own heart, this man's religion is vain.

Pure religion and undefiled before God and the Father is this, To visit the fatherless and widows in their affliction, and to keep himself unspotted from the world." — JAMES 1:26, 27.

LET US PRAY

Dear Jesus, — Help us to be sincere in all our endeavors to serve thee. Make us faithful to our Church, and our church school, and grant that we may learn how to do thy will by controlling ourselves.

When we would desire to say things that are mean, speak to us that we may hold back the words that our tongues might be about to say.

Grant, too, that we may have a forgiving heart when our friends say mean things to us when we know they really don't mean them.

Help our tongues not to "talk back" but to remember to "bridle" them. AMEN.

A PENDULUM

Back and forth, back and forth it swings.

Did you ever watch a pendulum swing back and forth in a grandfather's clock? It is real facinating. Good exercise for your head and neck. It is like watching a game of tennis — back and forth goes the ball, and your head with it.

Let's think about that pendulum a minute. It's always in motion but where does it go? Just from "here to there" and back again. Maybe that little weight on the end swings twelve or fifteen inches and back again, eight or ten thousand times or more each day. It seems to go nowhere in its hum-drum existence. Yet when you want to know what time it is you can run to the hall and look at the face on that clock and know that you are not late for school.

Speaking of school, you sort of imitate that pendulum, — you get up, wash your face, dress, eat breakfast, grab your things and off to school you go. You attend your classes and then come home; and then you do it all over again! It seems monotonous sometimes, doesn't it, even though you have a good time playing on the way, and when you get home.

However, like the pendulum, there is much more to it than just going and coming, back and forth. You see, you keep the school going, you keep the teachers working and at the end of the year you can look back at yourself and say "now I know more than I did a year ago!" And soon you can say "I'm ready for high school, and soon I'll be attending college! And then out earning vast sums of money." And I hope you will use that money to help less fortunate people in backward places so they can go to school and learn to be better citizens and be of greater service.

"The people gave heed to the words of Philip." — THE ACTS 8:6.

A MESSAGE FROM OUR BIBLE

"Therefore they that were scattered abroad went every where preaching the word.

Then Philip went down to the city of Samaria, and preached Christ unto them.

And the people with one accord gave heed unto those things which Philip spake, hearing and seeing the miracles which he did." — THE ACTS 8:4-8.

LET US PRAY

Dear God, — We thank thee for every opportunity that comes to us whereby we may show our willingness to be of service for thee. Keep us from thinking that doing our own pleasure is more important than doing thy will. Indeed, O God, grant that thy will may be our pleasure. Grant that our interest in the Church may give us the great purpose for our activities, and make us worthy Christians that what we do may bring other young people closer to thy way of life. AMEN.

A SPECK OF DUST

I presume most of you own a watch. You wake up in the morning and look at your watch. Maybe you get up and maybe you just lie back for another nap. It is the watch that tells you to hurry and get dressed for school.

Her watch probably tells the teacher when to ring the bell, and when to let you go out for recess, and to go home for lunch.

A watch is pretty important, especially when it keeps good time. When it is reliable you like to show it off, you are very proud of it. I might ask the question here, — Are you reliable, always? Are you trustworthy and dependable as you want your watch to be? Jesus was. Many people are.

One day the watch stopped. You tried winding it again. You shook it! But no use! So you finally took it to the repair shop and it was discovered that a tiny speck of dust had lodged in the delicate works and clogged the wheels.

That speck of dust was too small for you to see. The jeweler saw it only by using a magnifying glass. How you missed that watch! You hadn't realized how much you had come to depend upon it.

So it is, that people depend on you. They expect you to tell the truth. They expect you to be honest, and I hope nothing will ever keep you from being trustworthy. Keep your life and character clean and set it by the standard of Jesus. Like a good clean watch, seek to be accurate.

"Be an example of the believers." — TIMOTHY 4:12.

A MESSAGE FROM OUR BIBLE

"Let no man despise thy youth; but be thou an example of the believers, in word, in conversation, in charity, in spirit, in faith, in purity.

Till I come, give attendance to reading, to exhortation, to doctrine.

Take heed unto thyself, and unto the doctrine; continue in them; for in doing this thou shalt both save thyself, and them that hear thee. — 1 TIMOTHY 4:12, 13, 16.

LET US PRAY

Dear Lord, — I come to thee at the close of this happy day, to thank thee for the joy that has been mine in all my work and play.

Thank thee for my home and those who watch over me. Make me worthy of their love.

As I go to sleep and leave everything in thy care, I trust that all will be safe and have peaceful rest.

As the day dawns tomorrow, I ask for thy strength and peace that I, in turn, may impart joy to those about me. Guide me, O God, and give thy blessing to all. AMEN.

A PAIL OF WATER

On a farm in New Hampshire there is a well of clear, beautiful, tasteless water. The kind of water that one loves to drink when thirsty.

One morning everyone who drank that water noticed that it had a bitter taste, so we decided to wait a few days hoping that the fresh water, as it came into the well, would clear it up and make it all good and sweet again. But No! The well filled up and ran over but still the water was bad.

We then sent for a plumber and he pumped out all the water and cleaned the well thoroughly. This time the top of the well was covered, so that not even a tiny mouse could possibly fall in and drown!

Would you take a milk pitcher which was one third full of cream which had turned a wee bit sour, and fill it with sweet cream hoping thereby to make it *all* sweet?

Fresh cream won't sweeten sour cream. You can't make sour milk become sweet by pouring sweet milk in with it! You can't pour a pail of nice fresh clean water into a tub, half filled with muddy, soapy water, and make it good to drink!

And so boys and girls, just to SAY you are a Christian is not enough. You have to clean out the well! Every day pray to God to forgive you if you have said unkind words. Start saying nice things about people, but first ask them to forgive you if you have said wrong things. Clean out the mean thoughts you may have and then follow the teachings of Jesus when he said:

Cleanse first — the inside of the cup, that the outside may be clean also." — MATTHEW 23:26.

A MESSAGE FROM OUR BIBLE

"Woe unto you, scribes and Pharisees, hypocrites! for ye pay tithe of mint and anise and cummin and have omitted the weightier matters of the law, judgement, mercy, and faith; these ought ye to have done, and not to leave the other undone.

Ye blind guides, which strain at a gnat, and swallow a camel.

Woe unto you, hypocrites, for ye make clean the outside of the cup and of the platter, but within they are full of extortion and excess.

Thou blind Pharisee, cleanse first that which is within the cup and platter that the outside of them may be clean also. — MATTHEW 23:23-26.

LET US PRAY

Dear God, — We thank thee for being so patient with us, for sometimes we do not act or speak according to thy will. There are so many things we have neglected to do that we might have done in order to give happiness. In thy great love for us thou dost forgive. Make us worthy of thy forgiveness.

Even in the midst of his enemies Jesus refused to retaliate. We pray that we might be like him, and so be helpful in making peace and happiness real in the world.

Grant that thy love may be in our hearts that we may daily express it in our relationship with our friends. AMEN.

STETHOSCOPES

Did the doctor ever come to your house to see you? You were coughing real hard when you got up so mother kept you home from school and sent for the doctor to come and look at you.

When he arrived he examined you and asked a few questions and then took that "y" shaped rubber rope from his pocket. It looked something like a slingshot — but no, he put the two free ends, one in each of his ears, and the other end he placed at different parts on your chest.

Then he listened, and he heard the voices of the heart and the lungs speaking to him from inside the throat.

After his thorough examination he knew whether you should go to the hospital, or go back to bed, or just brace up and go to school.

That valuable three cornered rope detector is called a Stethoscope. Why do they use such big words for doctor's instruments? Because they have a real meaning. Divide that word and the dictionary will tell you that the first part means "breast or chest" and the second part means "spy or watch". It's the means by which the doctor "looks" inside your chest.

Prayer is a kind of stethoscope! When you pray to God earnestly you seem to hear Him telling you right from wrong. But you have to listen. Prayer is a listening device. We not only talk to God and ask him favors — we must listen and think carefully and then we will know his will. Let us listen with both ears. We can't talk to our friends and truly pray at the same time.

"Lord teach us to pray." — LUKE 11:1.

A MESSAGE FROM OUR BIBLE

"And it came to pass, that, as he was praying in a certain place, when he ceased, one of his disciples said unto him, Lord, teach us to pray, as John also taught his disciples.

I say unto you, Ask, and it shall be given you; seek, and ye shall find; knock, and it shall be opened unto you.

For every one that asketh receiveth; and he that seeketh findeth; and to him that knocketh it shall be opened." — LUKE 11:1, 9-10.

LET US PRAY

Our Father, — As thou didst send thy Son to us to show us how to live, so send us among our friends and to all in our school, to act and speak so that all may know thee better. We thank thee that through Jesus, thou hast taught us to pray. Whatever we ask in thy name thou wilt answer in a way that is best for us.

In all our little problems we ask thee to help us decide what is best, and thy interest in us gives us a feeling of security.

So may we, every day, many times, talk with thee, for in prayer we find guidance for our life. AMEN.

A BASEBALL BAT

A regulation baseball bat is one that is best suited to the user. Not every boy hits a home run every time he is up. He just does the best he can with that bat.

Sometimes a sacrifice bunt is the best play, — he would like to swing that bat, but he must think of the team and do the best thing to win the game, even though he bunts and goes to the dug-out while another is slapped on the back when he crosses the plate!

We sometimes forget the boy with the bat.

You won't hit one thousand in every game — in fact you won't play at all in some games. But you are there in uniform ready, when needed.

Every boy and every girl has some ability along some line. He may not sing like Caruso but he can be up there singing in the chorus or just turning the pages for the organist. Some boys and girls seem to take the spotlight in class discussions at school, whereas Jimmy can't seem to force a word out! Yet Jimmy is right there with the right answers when questioned!

Maybe you won't get to swing the bat for a home run in the whole nine innings but you can be ready, all practiced up!

That is what God wants of you each day. Be ready. Be in uniform for Jesus. Keep in daily practice doing God's will by thoughtful acts and clean words and a happy disposition and, sometimes, by *sacrifice* of your own pleasure, and you will in the eyes of God and the world have an enviable batting average.

"Serve the Lord with gladness, come before his presence with singing." — PSALM 100:2.

A MESSAGE FROM OUR BIBLE

"Make a joyful noise unto the Lord, all ye lands.

Serve the Lord with gladness; come before his presence with singing.

Know ye that the Lord is God; it is he that hath made us, and not we ourselves, we are his people and the sheep of his pasture.

Enter into his gates with thanksgiving, and into his courts with praise; be thankful unto him and bless his name.

For the Lord is good; his mercy is everlasting; and his truth endureth to all generations." — PSALM 100.

LET US PRAY

Dear Father in Heaven, — we thank thee for the beauty that is around us and for the ability to enjoy it. We thank thee for showing us, in so many ways, thy love and care for us. Thou art good and thy mercy and help is ever ready for our use.

We praise thee, O God, for thy faith in us. Grant that our faith in thee will keep us trustworthy and thoughtful in heeding thy counsel to live according to the teachings and life of thy son Jesus.

Help us to be truly dependable and ready to be of service for thee. AMEN.

PEARLS

I guess you all know where pearls come from. A tiny grain of sand will get into a shell with an oyster. Just as it hurts your eye when sand blows into it, it irritates the oyster, so he wraps a film around it, and eventually that becomes a pearl.

When I see a string of pearls, I think of the suffering of those oysters and how hard they worked to cover over that little grain of sand with a slimy film that finally hardened into a smooth round surface.

Some pearls are beautiful and brilliant in color, and some are just a dull covered-over grain of sand.

Now pearls seem to be most valuable when they are matched with other pearls. One pearl handled knife is beautiful but six or a dozen matched, handpicked knives are almost invaluable, breathlessly lovely. It is the same with a string of pearls, it is most valuable when the beads match each other in color and brilliance.

People, like pearls, are most valuable when they work and play and serve happily with other folks. Jesus was a friend to all and He wanted all people to work with Him to make this a Christian world.

Just as a string of pearls is beautiful so this community and the world will be more peaceful and happy if each of us will try to match our lives with Christ's in our service and thoughtfulness towards others.

"The Kingdom of God is like unto a man seeking pearls, who when he found one, sold all that he had and bought it." — MATTHEW 13:45-46.

A MESSAGE FROM OUR BIBLE

"Again the kingdom of heaven is like unto a merchantman, seeking goodly pearls;

Who, when he had found one pearl of great price, went and sold all that he had, and bought it. — MATTHEW 13:45-46.

LET US PRAY

Dear Jesus, — Help us keep from all jealousy and envy. Grant that it may be in our hearts to share what we have, and bring happiness to others.

Guide us to so live as to match our lives with Christ's and be able to, thereby, make our world a happier place for all.

We ask thee to bless the children of other lands, especially the less fortunate and the distressed. Grant that we may show thy spirit of love by sharing with them a portion of our abundance.

We ask thee to bless the Missionaries who are preaching thy message to those who do not know thee, and grant that all children may learn of thee. AMEN.

FOUNDATIONS

In the Bible, this word "foundations" appears many times. Jesus is referred to as the foundation upon which we should build our lives.

A foundation is that part of the structure which supports the rest of the building. Therefore if the foundation is weak then the parts which it holds up will begin to sag and twist and finally may fall.

Do you sometimes stub your toe as you walk along the sidewalk? Some sidewalks are so twisted and rough it makes you dizzy to look at them. You see, the foundation of gravel and sand wasn't deep enough so the frost of winter caused it to heave. Therefore, it had to be dug up and laid again.

Sometimes buildings will sag at one corner because of a poor foundation corner stone.

Jesus is referred to as the corner stone set on a firm foundation, upon which we should conduct our lives. That is, we should listen to his counsel and follow his teachings. By following his example we will be strong in character and the world will be safe and strong.

Jesus taught us to go to Church. He taught us to pray. The Church, prayer and worship, — these are foundations upon which our community will safely live in peace and happiness and in trust towards one another.

"He laid the foundation upon a rock." — LUKE 6:48.

A MESSAGE FROM OUR BIBLE

"And why call ye me, Lord, Lord, and do not the things which I say?

Whosoever cometh to me and heareth my sayings, and doeth them, I will shew you to whom he is like;

He is like a man which built an house, and digged deep, and laid the foundation on a rock; and when the flood arose, the stream beat vehemently upon that house, and could not shake it; for it was founded upon a rock.

But he that heareth, and doeth not, is like a man that without a foundation built an house upon the earth; against which the stream did beat vehemently, and immediately it fell; and the ruin of that house was great." — LUKE 6:46-49.

LET US PRAY

Dear Lord, — We thank thee for the certainty of thy love towards us. We know thou art good. Help us to grow to be more like thee in thy goodness. We have complete faith in thy love for us. Grant that we may keep thee always in our thoughts that our love for others may be expressed daily.

As thou art trustworthy, teach us to be so. May the example of thy kindness always be in our minds that we may always speak well of others, and act towards them as Jesus would do.

Help us to always be ready to answer thy call for helpers to do thy will. AMEN.

SHINGLES

When I was a little boy on the farm in Bath, N. H., I used to like to try to do everything my father did. But, you see, he was quite a bit older than I and a lot more experienced, so after I had tried and made mistakes I would let him show me the right way. I find that is a pretty good idea; let someone who knows teach us the right way, then what we do will be good examples to others.

Well, anyway, I remember my father started to shingle the barn roof, so one day I climbed up the ladder all the way to the roof and after watching Dad nail on a few shingles I started in. Fortunately my father was watching me, for pretty soon he came over and showed me that I couldn't just nail the shingles one beside the other, I was supposed to "break joints" with the row beneath, in other words each shingle had to over lap the ones beneath so the rain wouldn't leak through the cracks. So, you see, all the shingles on the roof worked together to keep out the rain and melting snow and even the cold winds of winter.

I think that is a very good lesson we all should learn. We can't just go our own way and do as we please all the time. We have to "break joints" with other people. It takes more than one person to play baseball or football or any game. Each boy or girl has to cooperate with the others, cover the empty spaces so the ball can't get through.

Furthermore, we all need friends and the way to make friends is to be one. Be unselfish, be kind to the unfortunate and considerate to those who seem to be shy or unpopular. This will keep out the storms of discord and hatefulness and wrong doing. Show yourself friendly to all.

"— *strive together for the Faith of the Gospel.*" — PHILIPPIANS 1:27.

A MESSAGE FROM OUR BIBLE

"Only let your conversation be as it becometh the gospel of Christ; That whether I come and see you, or else be absent, I may hear of your affairs, that ye stand fast in one spirit, with one mind striving together for the faith of the gospel.

For unto you it is given in the behalf of Christ, not only to believe on him, but also to suffer for his sake;

Having the same conflict which ye saw in me, and now hear to be in me." — PHILIPPIANS 1:27, 29-30.

LET US PRAY

Dear Jesus, — Thou hast taught us that forgiveness is very important but sometimes we find it very difficult to overlook words that have been said about us which are not true. Help us to think of other things, so, when a request for forgiveness comes to us we may be ready and willing to forgive.

So many wrong things were said to thee and about thee, yet thou didst bear no grudge. May love rule in our lives as it did in thine. AMEN.

TONGUES

I suppose nearly every boy has a cart; and to steer it he takes hold of the little stick or rod that is attached to the axle between the two front wheels.

Once in a while, even in this day of motor trucks, you will see a big cart drawn by two horses. Between them, and with one end attached to the cart, is the same stick or pole. This is called a tongue, and by it the heavy truck is steered.

Sometimes the road is rough and the tongue jerks back and forth banging against the sides of the horses. They don't like this and often just quit and refuse to budge, and the load doesn't get to its destination on time!

I've seen two horses trying to pull a heavy load, but they didn't work together, — first one would start and then the other, and that tongue would wag back and forth slapping against the shoulders of the horses.

But when the horses pull together the tongue remains steady and does no harm.

Does your tongue ever wag and hurt someone?

When things go wrong, and someone doesn't agree with you, does your tongue start acting up? Does it slap at this person, saying things that hurt? It hurts you, too, for the tongue slaps back!

It is much better to cooperate with others, to pull together, for when you do, everything goes smoothly, no one gets hurt and everyone is happy.

"The tongue is a little member —." — JAMES 3:5.

A MESSAGE FROM OUR BIBLE

"For in many things we offend all. If any man offend not in word, the same is a perfect man, and able also to bridle the whole body.

Behold, we put bits in the horses' mouths, that they may obey us; and we turn about their whole body.

Behold also the ships, which though they be so great, and are driven by fierce winds, yet are they turned about with a very small helm, whithersoever the governor listeth.

Even so the tongue is a little member, and boasteth great things. Behold how great a matter a little fire kindleth!"
— JAMES 3:2-5.

LET US PRAY

Dear God, — Help us to keep our tongue under control at all times. We are grateful to thee for the example of kindness and thoughtfulness which thou didst show at all times. Thy words of wisdom have directed us to a better life. Keep us from saying cross words, that we may not be offensive towards those with whom we play.

Help us, in our homes, to be thoughtful and to keep from saying anything that will hurt those whom we love. AMEN.

THE BLACKSMITH

I love to watch a blacksmith. When I was a boy I used to run in to his shop just to watch the sparks fly! They seemed to fly all over the big man, but he didn't seem to mind. They were such tiny sparks that, I guess, they didn't burn through his leather apron.

Suddenly one day a story came to me about a blacksmith who lived many years ago. As Joseph and Mary found "no room" in the Inn they stopped at a blacksmith's shop — but he was very busy and said "Be on your way, I am making nails to crucify the Messiah who is soon to be born." That night the Christ Child was born in a manger, in a stable.

In the morning there came a little girl, slowly and carefully walking up the street. Mary noticed her and took her by the hand and asked her to come in and see the tiny baby. The girl said "I cannot, for I am blind." But Mary led her to the crib and the little girl touched the Baby and immediately she could see! She jumped with joy and ran to her father — the blacksmith.

The blacksmith was so over-joyed he left his work and came to the stable Manger and threw himself on his knees and prayed God to forgive him.

He also asked Joseph and Mary to forgive him, saying — "If I had only known, you could have had my whole house last night."

Joseph spoke kindly to the big blacksmith and told him to go back to his work in peace. This he did and made only horseshoes, and hammered no more on nails to crucify the Messiah! If he had only known as we know now!

"Unto you a child is born." — LUKE 2:11.

A MESSAGE FROM OUR BIBLE

"And there were in the same country shepherds abiding in the fields, keeping watch over their flock by night.

And, lo, the angel of the Lord came upon them, and the glory of the Lord shone round about them; and they were sore afraid.

And the angel said unto them, Fear not; for, behold, I bring you good tidings of great joy, which shall be to all people.

For unto you is born this day in the city of David a Saviour, which is Christ the Lord." — LUKE 2:8-11.

LET US PRAY

Dear Jesus, — We thank thee for thy life. We are grateful for thy teachings of love and generosity. Thou didst love us enough to die for us, in order that we might know how to conduct our lives.

Help us to live in peace with one another, to work and play without selfishness or discord.

As we give gifts to our friends, may our greatest gift be our friendship. As we give gifts to our parents, and brothers and sisters may our love be of most importance. AMEN.

CHRISTMAS

I wonder if you have any friends in Christmas, Lawrence Co., Kentucky.

There are a number of towns named Christmas in the United States. There is a Christmas in Arizona, Gala Co. Another in Orange Co., Florida, also there is a Christmas in Bolivar Co., Mississipppi, and one in Roane County, Tennessee. So, you see, people who live in these States have Christmas the year round.

Perhaps some day, you will go fishing in Christmas Lake in Scott Co., Minnesota; or visit Christmas Island in the Pacific Ocean as did Captain Cook on Christmas day 1777 and so gave it that name.

But as for me and my friends Christmas is right where we are if we have the spirit of Jesus in our hearts.

Did you know that the Christmas seal idea came from Denmark? In 1904 there was a great need for a children's hospital in the city of Copenhagen, and Eimar Holboell, a postal clerk, thought of the idea of decorating letters and packages at Christmas time with colored seals and using the income of their sale for this hospital fund.

Jacob Riis in America, interested in social service, received a letter from his mother country with one of these seals on it. He wrote about it in a magazine (The Outlook), and a Miss Emily O. Bissell of Wilmington, Delaware organized the first sale of such seals in the United States for tuberculosis victims. From 1908 to 1920 the Red Cross worked in conjunction with the tuberculosis Association and since 1920 has carried on the sale alone.

The spirit of Christmas has indeed, been the inspiration of great service in the world. So when you receive those many gifts on Christmas day ask yourself "What have I done for God? How much have I given of my services to others, especially to those in need?" Remember what Jesus said and how He lived —

"It is better to give than to receive." — THE ACTS 20:35.

A MESSAGE FROM OUR BIBLE

"And now, brethren I commend you to God, and to the word of his grace, which is able to build you up, and to give you an inheritance among all them which are sanctified.

I have coveted no man's silver, or gold, or apparel.

I have shown you all things, how that so labouring ye ought to support the weak, and to remember the words of the Lord Jesus how he said, It is more blessed to give than to receive.

And when he had thus spoken, he kneeled down and prayed with them all." — THE ACTS 20: 32-36.

LET US PRAY

Father in Heaven, — Please give us generous hearts that, as we know of hungry children in the world, we may sacrifice, if necessary, in order to give for their need.

We thank thee for thy love which causes us to stop and think that it is much better to give to others than to always be thinking about what we may receive. Guide us, we pray. AMEN.

THANKSGIVING

Thanksgiving day is always an occasion to which we look forward. There are two good reasons, — one is that it is a school holiday, the other is that there will be plenty of good things to eat, — turkey with all the fixins'!

But there is something else about Thanksgiving that seems far more important than playing and eating. I can best describe it by dividing the word.

First we are *thankful*.

If I should mention the things for which we are truly thankful, they would fill this page, — our homes, our parents, all our relatives, our church and school and our many friends, our country and above all the love of God and our ability to show that we love and honor him. Many, many other things would be on our list.

Secondly, *Giving* stands out as very important. Could you enumerate all the things your mother and father have given you? Don't count the spankings and scoldings they gave you, — you earned them!

They give you love and care and protection; they have given up many things for themselves in order that you might be happy and cared for. Their reward comes when they see you growing into fine Christian young men and women.

So we thank God for the spirit of giving. Yes we thank God FOR giving, — and those two last words form another important word "Forgiving." We often ask God to forgive us; Let us be ready to forgive one another as Jesus did.

We are glad that Sarah Hale appealed to three Presidents to set aside a Day of Thanksgiving and, finally, that Abraham Lincoln issued the first Proclamation recommending that people gather for Prayer in thanksgiving for God's goodness.

"Enter into his gates with thanksgiving — be thankful unto him." — PSALM 100:4.

A MESSAGE FROM OUR BIBLE

"Serve the Lord with gladness, come before his presence with singing.

Know ye that the Lord he is God; it is he that hath made us and not we ourselves; we are his people and the sheep of his pasture.

Enter into his gates with thanksgiving, and into his courts with praise: be thankful unto him and bless his name.

For the Lord is good; his mercy is everlasting; and his truth endureth to all generations." — THE PSALMS 100: 2-5.

LET US PRAY

Dear Lord, — We thank thee for our parents and for their watchful care. Help us never to hurt them by things we do or say. We thank thee for our teachers in Church and School. Help us always to think of their patience and love for us in all they do. We thank thee too for our Country and for the sacrifices many have made in the past to keep us free.

Bless other lands as well as ours in their hope that Christianity may soon bring peace on the earth among nations. AMEN.

A NINTH INNING HOMER

It is the World Series baseball game. It's the seventh, and therefore the last game. Whichever team wins this game, is the champion team of the year.

It's the ninth inning in this final game of the series which is all tied up three to three, and now the score in this last game is nine to nine with the Pirates going to bat in the last of the inning. Some sixty thousand people watched the first batter hit a home run and so win the series for Pittsburgh against New York. Bedlum broke loose, and you can imagine what happened, I guess Pittsburgh is still celebrating for winning a pennant after thirty five years.

To win means to prepare ourselves. I know a man who pushed a cart around, collected old rags and paper and iron, — almost anything. He now owns one of the largest trailer Vans in America with offices in five or six different cities. He did'nt just try to beat somebody, he simply wanted to win. Not everybody can "beat" everybody — but everyone can be a winner.

—To me, winning is a matter of training one's self, — so living day by day, not hoping to beat some one but trying to master one's self.

Jesus is the clear cut example of a winner. He didn't win the argument with Pilate or with those who sought to crucify Him, but in the eyes of God and of men today, He was a real winner.

We may lose a skirmish now and then, but if our life is right and our hope and faith is in God, we will always be winners, for sometimes

"The race is not to the swift, nor the battle to the strong —" ECCLESIASTES 9:11.

A MESSAGE FROM OUR BIBLE

"Whatever thy hand findeth to do, do it with thy might; for there is no work, nor device nor knowledge, nor wisdom, in the grave.

I returned, and saw under the sun, that the race is not to the swift, nor the battle to the strong, neither yet bread to the wise, nor yet riches to men of understanding, nor yet favour to men of skill; but time and chance happeneth to them all.

Wisdom is better than weapons of war; but one sinner destroyeth much good." — ECCLESIASTES 9:10-11, 18.

LET US PRAY

Dear God, — Grant that we may be able to keep physically fit so that we may be strong and athletic. But as we think about the physical things we like to do, make us remember to keep our minds fit so that we will grow in knowledge and wisdom. But more important please talk to us when the temptation of cheating or telling an untruth comes to our thoughts, and keep us spiritually strong enough to resist any temptation.

We pray thee, help us keep clean hearts. AMEN.

WHY SPARKS FLY

Some day when you can't think of anything to do ask your dad, when he isn't too busy, to take you to a blacksmith's shop. There are not many around in these days, but there just might be one in your town.

A blacksmith shop is where a man takes a piece of iron and makes useful things out of it, such as shoes for horses, or most anything that is made of iron.

First the blacksmith will heat the piece of iron and then take it by a pair of tongs, place it upon an anvil, and with a heavy hammer he will pound it into the shape he desires.

I always used to like to go with my father, to the blacksmith's shop just to see the sparks fly.

The sparks flew in every direction, every time the Smithy struck a blow with his hammer. They flew on him and all around him. It was really a beautiful sight.

What made all those sparks fly? Sure, the iron was hot but there were no sparks until he hit it! As he struck the piece of hot iron the pressure of the blow caused the atoms in the iron to explode and the hot sparks flew out. The heat and pressure power from within the iron caused the sparks to fly.

The Anvil, upon which the iron was placed to be shaped, is mentioned only once in the Bible. But it shows how we must help each other shape our lives aright. The power is within us, — the power of love and kindness and faith in God. As we practice that power in our work and play with other boys and girls, it will influence them to talk and act as Jesus would like them to. Your words and acts are like the sparks that fly from the power within, to give beauty and joy to others and thereby helping them shape their lives.

He "smote the anvil — " ISAIAH 41:7.

A MESSAGE FROM OUR BIBLE

"They helped everyone his neighbour; and every one said to his brother, Be of good courage.

So the carpenter encouraged the goldsmith, and he that smootheth with the hammer him that smote the anvil, saying, it is ready for the soldering; and he fastened it with nails, that it should not be moved." — ISAIAH 41 : 6, 7.

LET US PRAY

Dear Lord, — Keep me from being lazy. As thou dids't go about doing good, help me to be good that I may best be of service to thee.

Keep me from putting things off, lest they don't ever get done. Teach me how to be more worthy of thy great love and to be dependable in thy service, and have the courage to express my Christian convictions. AMEN.

A YOKE

I remember, when I was a boy, my father wanted to plow a field which had never been plowed before and therefore it was very tough to turn the sod. So Dad bought a pair of oxen!

Now you can not harness an ox as you do a horse and hitch two together as easily. All they have is a yoke.

This yoke does two things, — it allows the oxen to pull the load, and to pull together. It is a heavy piece of wood so shaped as to fit the neck and shoulders of the oxen. This, of course holds the animals together. Then with a long chain we hitched the plow to the middle of the yoke between the two oxen and with a short stick I poked and prodded the oxen very lightly and urged them to start walking, which they did, and the plow, with my father at the handles, did the work of turning over the tough turf of the field. They seemed to do it so easily. The yoke fitted their shoulders and they pulled together.

I was interested in watching two sisters trying to get out of doing some work around the house which they were asked to do. People waste more valuable time trying to get *out* of work than it would take to do it. One girl would keep saying "Its your turn" and the other came back with "No, it's your turn to do it today. I did it yesterday", — and so it went on and on, until someone stepped in and told them *both* to do it. Working together the task was quickly, and easily done; and they were out playing in no time.

That is the way Jesus wants us to do His work of establishing peace and love and goodness in the world around us. Pull the load and pull together and thus make the burden easy. Remember what Jesus said:

"My yoke is easy and my burden is light." — MATTHEW 11:30.

A MESSAGE FROM OUR BIBLE

"Come unto me all ye that labour and are heavy laden, and I will give you rest.

Take my yoke upon you and learn of me; for I am meek and lowly in heart; and ye shall find rest unto your souls.

For my yoke is easy, and my burden is light."— MATTHEW 11:28-30.

LET US PRAY

Dear Jesus, — As thou dids't pray, teach us to pray. Help us overcome our jealousies and personal desires, that our thoughts may be more for others. We ask for thy strength that we may help others in need.

Make us humble and free from conceit as we turn to thee in prayer, that thy blessing may flow through our hearts to those around us. AMEN.

OVER THE HILL
Contributed by Robert H. Sargent.

Have you ever noticed, as you were driving along the road, that the closer you got to a hill that looked so very steep when you saw it from a few miles away, the less steep it seemed to become? And finally, when you arrive at the hill itself, it doesn't seem steep at all.

I may notice this more because I have a small four cylinder car, and it sometimes slows down as it climbs a steep hill. It doesn't have quite as much power as a big eight cylinder car would have. So I notice the hills as I approach them and hope they aren't too steep for my little car.

I have yet to come to a hill I cannot make, — they seem to shrink as I get closer to them.

I have noticed that trouble seems to be the same way. When I look at trouble which I expect to come in the near future, I get a little worried wondering if I will be able to handle it and "make the grade." But when the trouble finally arrives, it seems to have shrunk. Just like the hill, the closer you get to trouble, the smaller it seems to be. If this is the case, then there isn't much sense worrying about things that "might" happen.

There is a saying in our fiftieth state which tells us, "If you look trouble in the face, it will either go away, or it will stick around and be friendly like everything else."

So don't be afraid you won't make the grade. Mountains shrink to mole hills; hills shrink to inclines when you meet them head on, unafraid, with faith in God, our Creator and Sustainer.

"Therefore do not be anxious about tomorrow, — Let the day's own trouble be sufficient for the day." — MATTHEW 6:34.

A MESSAGE FROM OUR BIBLE

"I say unto you, take no thought for your life, what ye shall eat, or what ye shall drink; nor yet for your body, what ye shall put on. Is not the life more than meat, and the body more than raiment?

Seek ye first the kingdom of God, and his righteousness; and all these things shall be added unto you.

Take therefore no thought for the morrow; for the morrow shall take thoughts for the things of itself. Sufficient unto the day is the evil thereof." — MATTHEW 6: 25, 33-34.

LET US PRAY

Dear Lord, — We thank thee for a pleasant day, and for the fun we have had. We thank thee for the opportunities that have been ours whereby we have been useful.

Help us to be worthy of thy love as we look forward to another day in which we may help others, and not think only of ourselves. So please give us willing hearts to express thy will in our everyday work and play. AMEN.

WINDSHIELDS

Every automobile has a windshield. Most cars have from three to six windows. Now, those windows and windshields are made of glass for one particular reason, to see through. Wood or steel would keep out the wind and cold and rain even better than glass, but how would Dad see to drive? How could you and mother look out at the scenery and see the very beautifully colored leaves in the Fall which decorate our highways?

I got into my car the other day and someone remarked how dingy the windshield and windows were, and do you know, things outside looked dingy too, especially the bright red and yellow leaves on a particularly beautiful tree just across the street. How dull and colorless those leaves looked through that dingy windshield! Perhaps I wouldn't have noticed it so much, only for the fact that the next time I used the car I could see that the leaves looked far more brilliant. They were the same leaves but someone had cleaned the windshield!

Some days are like the dingy windshield, cloudy and foggy and it seems to make everyone unhappy, — and then God seems to tell the sun to clean it all away, and what a difference it makes.

Sometimes boys and girls get out of sorts and dingy looking, — they call it being grouchy, — just because mother wants an errand done, or because you can't watch your favorite program on T.V. When you find things aren't going to your liking, stop and say a little prayer and ask God to help you clean that sour feeling from your mind with a feeling of love and thoughtfulness, and see how much brighter everything looks and how much happier you see other people become.

"He that hath clean hands and a pure heart." — PSALM 24:4.

A MESSAGE FROM OUR BIBLE

"Who shall ascend unto the hill of the Lord? or who shall stand in his holy place?

He that hath clean hands and a pure heart; who hath not lifted up his soul unto vanity nor sworn deceitfully.

He shall receive the blessing from the Lord, and righteousness from the God of his salvation." — THE PSALMS 24: 3-5.

LET US PRAY

Oh God, — keep me trustworthy at all times. Help me keep my promises and grant that, as opportunities come, thou wilt find me dependable in service.

Teach me thy will, O God, and, through me, help the children of other lands who are hungry and cold.

May the warmth of thy love in me give them courage by my concern and thoughtfulness. AMEN.

OARS

I wonder if you boys and girls know what oars are? O, you do. That's fine, because they have a lot to say to us in this Parable today. I guess most boats in these days have a motor attached, but occasionally a boat is operated only by oars. So lets take a ride in one of these oar-driven boats!

After you have rowed around the Lake a while you get tired and you "lie on the oars", which means you lift the oars out of the water and stop working. That leaves your friend who is rowing with you, to do all the work.

Then sometimes, even though you know you should be back in camp you "boat your oars" and just lie there in the boat, while mother is waiting dinner for you.

I have also seen people try to row with just one oar. Well, you know what happens, you row on and on and pretty soon you are right back where you started. You just couldn't reach the place you headed for.

Just as sure as these wooden oars are necessary to make that little boat go where you want it to, so, more important, are the spiritual oars of your religion in making your life go in the right direction and toward the right goal.

Your knowledge and love for Jesus will direct you to being a great man or woman. Taking hold of the church with all your might and working for it, will help you reach the right goal. Never "lie on your oars" or "boat your oars", don't leave tasks that need to be done, for someone else to do. Keep both oars, all your strength and ability working for Jesus.

"*—but she cast in all that she had.*" — LUKE 21:4.

A MESSAGE FROM OUR BIBLE

"And he looked up, and saw the rich men casting their gifts into the treasury.

And he saw also a certain poor widow casting in thither two mites.

And he said, Of a truth I say unto you, that this poor widow hath cast in more than they all;

For all these have of their abundance cast in unto the offerings of God; but she of her penury hath cast in all the living that she had." — LUKE 21 : 1-4.

LET US PRAY

Our Heavenly Father, — Help us to think correctly as young people today. Although we may sometimes, be confused in mind, we are sure of thy spiritual strength to guide us aright.

Grant that we may always keep our thoughts upon thee, O God, that we may be generous and kind, — thoughtful of other peoples' needs.

Bless all young folks that friendliness and good will may come into the world of all nations. AMEN.

A LITTLE GOLF BALL

Some time ago I watched a golf tournament, and as those expert players each hit that little ball with a beautiful swing, I could see it go straight down the fairway toward the green, and finally stop about two hundred and fifty yards away. And then, on the green, I saw those men putt that ball ten, fifteen and even twenty feet and it would often roll straight into the little cup.

Of course I give most of the credit to the man who hits the ball, but at the same time I wondered why a golf ball should go farther and straighter than a small pumpkin or a hickory nut or a marble! So I inquired.

Golf balls used to be made with a tiny solid rubber ball in the center but later it was found that this inner little ball, (not solid rubber), could be filled with an acid liquid. This liquid was forced into it and then the outer wrappings were wound around it. But this inner ball had to be accurately in the center of the golf ball. The slightest degree off center would cause the ball to wobble. Because of the liquid forced into the center of the ball it would go straight and far, IF the man who hit it did so squarely and followed through.

So it seems to me this game of golf can show us much about the way of living. First we must have an idea of the goal we seek to reach. Is our goal just "distance" or do we have a designated "Green and cup" as our hope. God has set for us a great hope — The life and teachings of Jesus Christ. If we *fill* our lives with the love of God; if we continually practice the teachings of Jesus, doing the very best we can as we go up the fairway of our career, we will find happiness and a sense of well being, and true direction.

"As many as are led by the spirit of God, these are sons of God." — ROMANS 8:14.

A MESSAGE FROM OUR BIBLE

"For as many as are led by the spirit of God, they are the sons of God.

The spirit itself beareth witness with our spirit, that we are the children of God.

And if children, then heirs; heirs of God, and joint heirs with Christ; if so be that we suffer with him, that we may be also glorified together." — ROMANS 8: 14, 16-17.

LET US PRAY

O Lord, — direct us in all we do, and guide the direction of our lives. Grant us thy continual help that, in our works, we may express our deep faith in thee and express our love for thee as thy loyal children. AMEN.

NO SISSIES HERE
Contributed by Robert H. Sargent

In 1960, at a place called Sqaw Valley, California, an event took place that happens only every four years. It was called the Winter Olympics. As you know, this is a time when top athletes from all over the world come together to compete in the Olympic Games.

Perhaps you watched some of the activities on television. If so, you may recognize the names, — Barbara Lockhart, Jeanne Ashworth, or Ted Farwell. These were three of the United States' entrants.

Many of us might day-dream about what we would do if we were among the top athletes of the world, representing our country in this greatest of all sports events. When we day-dream like this we think of the glory that could be ours, but often we overlook the years of training which goes into making up these great athletes.

Barbara Lockhart, who competed in the 1500 meter women's speed skating event, Jeanne Ashworth, who scored an upset victory for the United States by placing third in the 500 meter women's speed skating event, and Ted Farwell, a cross-country skier, all attended the newly built United Church at Sqaw Valley. During the few weeks they were there, they took part in informal discussion groups and evening services. They helped in leading one of the special Olympic Services.

These are not only great athletes, they are Christian young people. In the words of Barbara Lockhart: "We committed ourselves in confidence to do our best with honor and true sportsmanship, and to seek the greatest prize — 'to give glory to Thy great Name in the service of thy Christ'." If Christianity can be so meaningful to some of the top athletes of the world, we surely should be eager to speak out about our faith and our association with the Christian Church.

"Be strong in the grace that is in Christ Jesus" — 2 TIMOTHY 2:1.

A MESSAGE FROM OUR BIBLE

"Thou therefore, my son, be strong in the grace that is in Christ Jesus.

And the things that thou hast heard of me among many witnesses, the same commit thou to faithful men, who shall be able to teach others also.

Thou therefore endure hardness, as a good soldier of Jesus Christ." — 2 TIMOTHY 2: 1-3.

LET US PRAY

Dear Father, — I thank thee for all the beauty of things around me that thou hast made. I am happy when I think of thee as my Father who loves me and cares for me.

Forgive me for any wrong I may have done today and make me strong in spirit that I may do better tomorrow, and so live as to teach thy love and make it real among us as we play and work. AMEN.

NAMES

I wonder if you know the meaning of your name. If you do not, I suggest that you look it up in a dictionary. Of course the meaning may not apply to you. On the other hand, when you know the meaning of your name, you might like to live up to it — if you like it! For instance, is your name Albert? That means "illustrious". Perhaps some day you will be!

The name Guy means "a leader" — I'm sure that is a good name to live up to. Henry means "chief". Paul means "small" — I believe we gather from the Bible that Paul was small of stature.

I guess you all know that Peter means "Rock", and Andrew means "strong". Both these men of the Bible were strong men of character. Matthew and John both seem to have the meaning of "God's gift". Mark means "polite" and Luke has the meaning of "light".

I like the legends of Indian names. It is said that an Indian by the name of Susqua used to go out evenings, exploring the rapids of a great river. Sometimes he would be late coming home and his good wife used to get pretty nervous about his safety. At such times, she would go out to the river bank and call to him in a loud voice: "Susqua, Susqua, Susqua." Soon her mind would be at ease for she would hear the answer as he called her name: "Hanna, Hanna", and so the name was given to the Susquehanna river!

What a very lovely and appropriate name is Jesus which means Saviour. He certainly lived his whole life as a saviour of men in trouble, teaching all people how to live right, by his own example.

God also gave him the name of Christ as He appointed, "anointed", Him to represent Him among the people of the earth.

I hope you boys and girls are all true Christians, "Followers of Jesus Christ" And that you will always live up to the meaning of that word "Christian."

"Thou shalt call his name Jesus" — LUKE 1:31

A MESSAGE FROM OUR BIBLE

"—Thou shalt call his name Jesus.

He shall be great, and shall be called the Son of the Highest; and the Lord God shall give unto him the throne of his father David.

And he shall reign over the house of Jacob for ever; and of his kingdom there shall be no end." — LUKE 1: 31-33.

LET US PRAY

Our Heavenly Father, — We thank thee for our Bible and the teachings that Jesus gave us to show us how to live.

There are many things we do not understand, but thy love, as expressed by Jesus, can easily be felt. Grant that we all may apply the meaning of the word "Christian" to our lives; so act and speak that all may know we try to follow thy counsel.

Make us worthy of thy love and teach us to always be honest with one another. AMEN.

RUTS

Did you ever go tobogganing? If you have tried it, you know that the toboggan goes faster after the first few times. Also, after the first few times, the toboggan steers better because a path, or rut, has been formed.

However, when you are riding your bicycle you want to keep out of ruts, for if you don't you are liable to get a good spill. I imagine you have more than one scar to show for the "header" you may have taken.

So you see there are two kinds of ruts, — some are good and some are bad for us.

I love a railroad train, — especially the steam engine kind that show their power by their puffing. It is amazing to me how they keep on those narrow tracks, mile after mile, with very few accidents. I like to call those rails inverted or down-side-up ruts! At least they hold the train in place and give safe passage to the passengers.

When the Indians wanted to go from place to place they cut a trail through the woods, usually near a stream, and these trails became well trodden ruts or paths over a period of time.

In later years these trails were widened and became roads over which wagons were drawn, — and now they are paved into super-highways.

The habits you form are like ruts. Some are good and it may be that some are bad. Follow in the path that Jesus has set for you in his teachings, and keep using kind words, and being honest, and you will grow to be trustworthy men and women.

"I have chosen the way of Faithfulness" — PSALM 119:30.

A MESSAGE FROM OUR BIBLE

"Remove from me the way of lying—
I have chosen the way of truth; thy judgments have I laid before me.

Teach me O Lord, the way of thy statutes—
Give me understanding, and I shall keep thy law; yea, I shall observe it with my whole heart.

Make me to go in the path of thy commandments; for therein do I delight." — PSALM 119: 29-30, 33-35.

LET US PRAY

Dear Jesus — We thank thee that, because of thy example, we want to be trustworthy; through thy teachings our parents have led us to be honest. Keep us on the right course, in the path thou hast set for us.

Help those, dear Lord, who seem to fail to do what is right, and give them strength to abide by thy way of life. Please bless our homes and all who care for us. AMEN.

ICE

Contributed by Robert H. Sargent

One of the many past-times during the winter months, in the State of Maine, is ice fishing. When the ice is thick enough, cars, jeeps, and even small pick-up trucks drive out on it with all the equipment.

Usually the first thing that is done is to build a fire in such a way as not to melt the ice. Then a hole has to be chipped out through which to fish. To do this, a long iron pole, five or six feet long, with a sharp point on the end, is used. Then the lines are put through the holes and hooked up to what are called "tip-ups" so that when a fish takes the bait, and the hook, a red flag will tip up in the air to tell you that you have a fish, — you hope!

There are some people who don't like to go ice fishing. In fact, some people don't like ice! If you have ever stepped on a piece and fallen down, you probably don't like it either.

But if you depended on the number of fish you caught for a living, as the Indians do up here in Maine where I live, you would be thankful for ice, for during the winter the Indians can fish the whole lake, not just the shoreline, which they have to do in the summer unless they are fortunate enough to have a boat.

Another reason that they are thankful for ice is that they can use it for refrigeration to keep their fish from spoiling.

So you see, ice can be dangerous, or it can be a blessing. It can be used for good or bad purposes, depending on those using it and how it is used.

Our own lives can be used for good or bad purposes, depending on how we act and what we say. I hope you will faithfully study the life and teachings of Jesus, so that your life, like His, will always be used for good purposes.

"In all things showing thyself a pattern of good works." — TITUS 2:7.

A MESSAGE FROM OUR BIBLE

"Young men, exhort to be of a good mind.

In all things showing thyself a pattern of good works; in doctrine showing uncorruptness, gravity, sincerity.

Sound speech, that cannot be condemned; that he that is of the contrary part may be ashamed, having no evil thing to say of you.

Teaching us that we should live soberly, righteously, and godly, in this present world." — TITUS 2: 6-8, 12.

LET US PRAY

Dear God and Father of us all, — forgive our evil ways. May the inspiring faith, evidenced in the past, grow upon us, and add daily to our strength and determination to follow thy teachings.

As Jesus taught, always, to do thy will, O God, may we, under his guidance, seek to be worthy of sonship through thy care and love.

Bless the young people of our community and grant that our lives may be worthy examples, so that no one will be hurt by what we do or say. We ask thee to bless our homes, for Jesus' sake. AMEN.

IT'S TIME TO PAINT

A painter went out in the Spring looking for houses to paint. He made a bargain with one house owner. At first the owner thought the price was much too high, so the painter did some figuering and finally came up with the proposition that he could paint the house at a much cheaper cost. The owner was satisfied and the job was done in a very short time.

His neighbor thought it looked good so he called in the same painter. After talking with the man for a while they decided upon a price which was almost twice as much as the other house, but the painter first scraped the entire house; then he actually washed it with dirt remover. He mixed the paint and put on two coats.

Both houses looked very beautiful in their new dress!

After one year the first house began to peel in spots and the white paint looked yellowish in color, and after the third year the owner decided to have his house painted again. It looked so shabby in comparison with his neighbor's, for this second house looked as good and white and fresh as the day it was painted! For on this house the painter had worked hard. He scraped and washed away the old paint and the dirt that had gathered in the corners.

I was thinking that it is sometimes like that with people. When a boy or girl does something wrong, and someone suspects him, he might deny it, and try to cover it up, — perhaps by laying it on to someone else. But sooner or later everybody knows about it and the child feels pretty shabby.

The only honest and lasting way to do, if we do, or say something wrong, is to say "I'm sorry". Tell your friend that, and tell God too. Clean it from your conscience. Wash away all dirt, and God will put upon you a rich coat of righteousness which will be an honor to you and an admiration to all who know you.

"Stand therefore having your loins girt about with truth, — EPHESIANS 6:14.

A MESSAGE FROM OUR BIBLE

"Children, obey your parents in the Lord, for this is right.

Honor your father and mother; which is the first commandment with promise;

That it may be well with thee,

With good will, doing service, as to the Lord,

Take upon you the whole armour of God, that ye may be able to withstand in the evil day, and having done all, to stand.

Take the shield of faith, wherewith ye shall be able to quench all the fiery darts of the wicked. Praying always."
— EPHESIANS 6: 1-3, 7, 13, 16, 18.

LET US PRAY

Dear Lord, our Father, — Place within our hearts and minds the wisdom to do right, to be honest, and to realize thy way is truth. Bless our homes, dear God, and teach us to live on the sure foundation principles taught by Jesus.

Help parents to build for their children, those spiritual foundations that will remain with them throughout their whole lives. Give children the desire to always obey their parents, and help us all to keep our thoughts clean, and our hearts filled with thy love. AMEN.

POWER

I remember watching the engineers construct the well known "Camerford dam" at Fifteen-mile-falls on the Connecticut river just two or three miles from where I lived as a boy in Bath, N. H. In fact my father and I used to walk up through our back pasture, and another farm, and we were there! It was fun watching those great derricks and power machines at work building that huge dam.

Finally it was finished and the water rushed through the flumes and the wheels began to turn.

In Washington D. C. the President of the United States pushed a button and immediately power began to vibrate the wires that had been erected on great steel towers. These wires went all the way through our farm and on, for over one hundred sixty miles, to below the city of Lowell, Mass. The electric power was then to be distributed about the country to factories and homes.

However, even though the wires sing and pulsate with power, that energy is of no use until some one pulls a switch and lets the power in — to turn wheels, and to light lamps.

In God is the power and strength to make peace among nations and a good world, but it must flow through your life and mine before it can accomplish God's plans. He depends upon you to USE His power. We say and know, that "God is Love". But that power of love must energize your life, and you then must switch it into the lives of other boys and girls, before we can have complete happiness in the world. Prayer throws the switch that lets God's power of love into our lives and makes us want to distribute it all around us.

"Pray at all times, — be alert" — EPHESIANS 6:18.

A MESSAGE FROM OUR BIBLE

"Stand therefore, having your loins girt about with truth, and having on the breastplate of righteousness;

And your feet shod with the preparation of the gospel of peace;

And take the helmet of salvation, and the sword of the Spirit, which is the word of God;

Praying always with all prayer and supplication in the Spirit." — EPHESIANS 6: 14-15, 17-18.

LET US PRAY

Our Father, we thank thee for all the happiness that we have had, and grant that, as we think of all our blessings, we shall remember the young folks in the nations where homes have been destroyed, and where the lack of food is causing starvation.

Help us to follow Jesus' life, remembering how he went about doing good. Make us worthy of thy love, and give us the strength and the sense to do right in the face of any easy wrong; and may our example lead others to the right way. AMEN.

WINGS

What makes a bird fly and sail around upstairs in the sky? We immediately answer the question by saying "its wings". But no, it's the bird that makes him fly!

He sees a wormy apple at the top of a tree and he spreads his wings and makes them flap, and sails right to the target. The power in the bird's wings is in his desire to use them. Wings are just implements attached to the bird. God gave him the wings, and allowed them to grow, but the bird uses them, and the more he uses them the stronger they become.

What keeps an airplane up in the air? And makes it come down and land perfectly? The pilot! He pulls levers and pushes buttons and the wings of his 'plane obey him. Sometimes a plane "cracks up". The reason could be that the wings didn't obey the pilot. The guiding wing became broken and the pilot couldn't move it with his lever or his mechanical device.

A horse is very strong, but it is the driver who guides him with reins attached to a bit, which is in the mouth of the horse.

Do you have a power boat? How does it know where to go? There is a very small rudder in the water attached to the boat and you, or your father, moves it by means of a stick and wires hitched to it. It isn't the rudder that is most important, its *you* who moves it from side to side, and the boat goes where you want it to.

Well, how about it, when you get angry at someone do you start right in using your hands and fists, or do you let your brain tell your hands what to do? and so, keep out of trouble!

If you don't like what someone has said to you, do you start, right off, letting your tongue just wag, and say the first things that come to mind, for which you should, later, apologize? Or do you let your heart, and the fact that you are a Christian, take over and guide your tongue?

"*— guided by a small rudder, wherever the will of the pilot directs.*" — JAMES 3:4.

A MESSAGE FROM OUR BIBLE

"In many things we all offend, If any man offend not in word, the same is a perfect man, and able also to bridle the whole body.

Behold, we put bits in the horses' mouths, that they may obey us; and we turn about their whole body.

Behold, also the ships, which though they be so great, and are driven of fierce winds, yet are they turned about with a very small helm, whithersoever the governor listeth." — JAMES 3: 2-4.

LET US PRAY

"Our Heavenly Father, — Help us each day to become more Christ-like in spirit and in deeds. As we grow in stature, help us to grow also in wisdom and in thy favor. In so doing, grant that we may have the desire to show this Christian spirit towards those with whom we play.

We ask thee to give us patience in order that we may *think* before we speak, or act. Help us to be more thoughtful at home and at play. AMEN.

LIGHT

When I say "light" I wonder what you think of. What comes first to your mind? Maybe you just lost something on the floor and it rolled in back of a chair; so you ask for a flashlight! Or perhaps you are anxious to take an indoor picture with your brand new camera; so you go to the store and buy some flash bulbs. Possibly you are sitting in a dark corner of the room and are trying to read after the sun has gone down; so you pull a chain or turn a switch and you have more light.

Light is something that all the darkness in the world cannot extinguish. But a little candle's light can drive out darkness!

About the first thing you do when you go into a dark house or room, is to turn on the light. A gloomy looking room sure looks more cheerful and bright when the lights are on.

So it is with your home; If you are out in the evening, you can be sure that your mother and dad eagerly await your footsteps coming up the walk, and listen for the door to open and, believe me, your first words can make that home brighter or gloomy; happy or sad.

Do you come in sighing or laughing? Do you add light to the home? Are you cheerful and happy at a party, at school, at Church, thus helping to make everyone, and the very room itself seem brighter?

When you think of light, think also of *giving* it wherever you go. When we think of light I believe we often think of Jesus. People were glad to see Him. His personality conveyed light to the hearts of those who were discouraged and gloomy. So can you if you will follow his example. Indeed Jesus said so:

"Ye are the light of the world." — MATTHEW 5:14.

A MESSAGE FROM OUR BIBLE

"Ye are the light of the world. A city that is set on an hill cannot be hid.

Neither do men light a candle, and put it under a bushel, but on a candlestick; and it giveth light unto all that are in the house.

Let your light so shine before men, that they may see your good works, and glorify your Father which is in heaven," — MATTHEW 5: 14-16.

LET US PRAY

Dear Lord, bless the young folks of our community and make them thoughtful of others in their play, and in their desires.

Keep them from evil and all wrong doing, and grant that their homes may be happy because they bring cheer and joy into it.

Bestow thy kindness and pity upon those who, in other lands, as well as our own, are unhappy today. Touch our hearts that we may help bring joy and peace to their troubled minds and lives. We thank Thee for Jesus and his example of giving cheer and new light to people's lives. AMEN.

THE HUB

At the exact center of a wheel is the Hub. The next time you see a horse-drawn cart, or even a bicycle, just notice the wheels.

Out from, and around that hub the wheel is built. A dozen or more spokes are set into the Hub, and the other end of each spoke is attached securely to the outside rim, or felly, of the wheel. Sometimes you see the wheel of a cart, or your bicycle, start to wobble, and you wonder what is wrong! You examine the wheel and you find that one spoke is warped, or in the case of a wooden spoke, broken. This weakens the other spokes and causes the felly to be out of shape. So the spoke has to be straightened or replaced, and re-set securely into the Hub.

You know, I like to think of Jesus as the Hub of this human world, and Christian boys and girls as spokes securely fastened to Him and reaching out in all directions to help hold the world together, and make it solid, and smooth running, for God.

If at any time, during the week, at school or at play, you do, or say something that hurts someone, and things get sort of rough and you are left out of the games, try re-setting yourself into the Hub, and talk to God about it. Secure yourself to Jesus and He will give you strength to make things right again.

You see the hub needs the spokes to make the wheel run smoothly. So Jesus needs you. He needs your faithful allegiance to Him, that by your Church loyalty, and your prayers, your example will help keep others in a straight path to Righteousness so that — "All the nations shall come and worship before Thee", as prayed the PSALMIST 86:9.

A MESSAGE FROM OUR BIBLE

"All nations whom thou hast made shall come and worship before thee, O Lord; and shall glorify thy name.

For thou art great, and doest wondrous things: thou art God alone.

I will praise thee, O Lord my God, with all my heart: and I will glorify thy name for evermore.

For great is thy mercy toward me." — PSALM 86: 9-10, 12-13.

LET US PRAY

Heavenly Father, We thank thee for keeping us safe from danger through the night. Help us do nothing wrong today. Lead us to be kind and useful to all around us, and to be strong in our decisions against evil.

Keep us faithful, O Lord, in doing thy will, and speaking thy truth, that we may guide others to be closer friends of thine.

Please bless our homes and all who watch over us and all thy children everywhere. AMEN.

"evol zi boP"

A small boy was standing looking at a Church window. He had a very puzzled look on his face. He was getting into all sorts of positions, and even trying, almost, to stand on his head! He was trying to read what those words said that were written on the inside of that Church window.

A man came along and watched him a minute, and just as the boy was about to give up, he said to him, "You see, son, the reason you can't read that writing is because you are looking at it from the wrong side" "Come on in." So he took the boy into the Church, and they went to the window and they had no trouble reading those important words: "evol zi boP"

Can you get on the other side of those words?

We sometimes misjudge people, and we criticise them; we don't *try* to understand them, usually because we see only one side of the argument which is going on, — and it may be the wrong side! Before we "talk back" it is well to hear the other person's opinion. I remember, when riding on the Subway in New York an elderly woman was standing in front of a man who was seated. Some one made a remark about the man not rising to give the lady his seat. His face reddened but he remained seated. When his stop came, his wife came over from the back of the car and handed him his crutches and helped him to his feet and they left the train!

You know, I think the reason we do not always understand God, and see his love about us, is because we ourselves are on the wrong side. Prayer and worship is the key that lets us inside to have a clearer vision of trust, so that we can know what God wants to say to us.

When you get home take a mirror and get on the inside of those odd looking words and you will have the text for you to look up. — 1 JOHN 4:8.

A MESSAGE FROM OUR BIBLE

"We are of God; he that knoweth God heareth us; he that is not of God heareth not us. Hereby know we the spirit of truth, and the spirit of error.

Beloved, let us love one another; for love is of God; and every one that loveth is born of God, and knoweth God.

He that loveth not knoweth not God; for God is love.

In this was manifested the love of God toward us, because that God sent his only begotten Son into the world, that we might live through him." — 1 JOHN 4: 6-9.

LET US PRAY

We thank thee, dear Lord, that thy love has been made clear to us. Grant that we too may always be able to apply it in our every day life. Teach us to be patient when we see others doing wrong things, and saying unkind words, trying always to show them what is right.

We thank thee for the Church and the message of Jesus, and help us live by the teachings we have received. Bless our homes, dear God, and watch over us, every one. AMEN.